Fellowship

Fellowship

Lance Lambert

LANCE LAMBERT MINISTRIES

Richmond, Virginia, USA

ISBN: 978-1-68389-105-5

www.lancelambert.org

Contents

Introduction

During the summer of 1975, the first Christian Family Conference was held at Randolph Macon College in Ashland, Virginia. That week of fellowship and ministry of God's Word proved to be life changing for those in attendance.

One of the speakers, Lance Lambert, shared this at the beginning of his time of ministry: "What we need above everything else is to discover what God really means in practical terms by this statement of our Lord Jesus Christ: 'Upon this rock I will build my church and the gates of hell shall not prevail against it.'" He then shared seven messages on principles of fellowship from the Scripture, as well as from his experience at Halford House, Richmond, England. The content of those messages is printed in book form here for the first time.

1.
Principles of Fellowship

Isaiah 21:11–12

One calleth unto me out of Seir, Watchman, what of the night? Watchman, what of the night? The watchman said, The morning cometh, and also the night: if ye will inquire, inquire ye: turn ye, come.

Inquire of the Lord

This is a rather strange word to have: to inquire of the Lord, to behold the beauty of the Lord and to inquire in His temple. If ever there was a time in the history of God's people when we need to inquire of the Lord, surely it is now. We are standing, it seems to me, in the so-called free world, on the brink of tremendous catastrophe. It has only been the grace of God that has held back not only the flood of evil, but of war and of very much unhappiness. I believe that the Lord has held that back and given us all a breathing space. In the Yom Kippur War we came to the brink of world war. I do not think for a moment that the people in Europe or here in the States realized just how far that seemingly local, petty, Middle East War went. I believe that we have a time given to us in which we as the people of God might seek the Lord and know, because God will give us an understanding of His will, what it is that He requires of us today. You in America must surely bemoan the fact of Vietnam—56,000 of your best young lives thrown away with nothing whatsoever to show from it. We in Europe must wonder what is happening when Portugal, one of the bastions of our defence, has gone Communist, and when another bastion of our southern defence, Italy, is now under Communist administration in nearly every major city. I travel through the universities of Europe and Britain and Scandinavia and I see firsthand the battle for the souls of the nations being fought in the universities. It is hard to believe that things have gone so far in even conservative countries.

What has all of this got to do with us? Very much indeed. We do not know how long we have before we are all caught up in the vortex of some worldwide strife. In the breathing space that we have left to us we need to inquire of the Lord: "Watchman, what of the night? Watchman, what of the night?" The watchman said, "The morning comes and also the night." May God give us grace not to sleep through the morning that is given to us. There is a time of respite, a time of freedom, a time when we can work as we have never worked before, a time when we cannot only seek the will of God but find the will of God and do the will of God before that night comes when no man can work.

What are we to do? It is not only politically and economically that we see so much happening, but spiritually. We see some of those things, movements that I believe are the movements of the Spirit of God, which seem to hold so much promise within them of seeing the purpose of God fulfilled, going right off the rails one after another, systemized and fully alienated now from the real purpose of God. What are we to do? What is the purpose of the Lord for His people? I believe the purpose of God for us His people is the same purpose that He has always had for His people if we only had ears to hear.

Listen to the words of our Lord Jesus Christ in Matthew 16:18: "Upon this rock I will build my church; and the gates of Hell shall not prevail against it. I will give unto thee the keys of the kingdom of heaven: and whatsoever thou shalt bind on earth shall be bound in heaven; and whatsoever thou shall loose on earth shall be loosed in heaven."

What we need above everything else is to discover what God really means in practical terms by this statement of our Lord Jesus Christ. "Upon this rock I will build my church and the gates of hell shall not prevail against it." Why should we become the subject of devilish propaganda? Why should we, as it were, allow the enemy to impose upon us some idea that it is impossible, simply and not only because of political and economic conditions, but more so because we see so many things that have within it the promise of fulfilment going right off the road, right out of the way? Why should we allow the enemy to say that it is impossible? If our Lord Jesus said: "Upon this rock I will build My church," and added for our comfort and strengthening, "and the gates of hell shall not prevail against it," then I for one say the gates of hell are not going to prevail against it. We need to inquire of the Lord as to what He means.

The burden that I have in my heart is very simple. It is to do with fellowship, true fellowship. In the times that I have, by the grace of God, I will seek to speak about principles of fellowship, unless He completely changes the whole course. I hope that God will help us to get right down to some of those practicalities about fellowship. We desperately need to know what fellowship is. For the most part, the people of God do not know what fellowship is. They have false ideas about it. They do not understand the principles that govern fellowship, and because of this so often they are at sea spiritually. Although we may grow individually, we never really see this being built together in Christ as a habitation of God in the Spirit. That is my burden.

I believe that in Zechariah 4 we have in many ways the key to our present dilemma, and for many of you it is a well-known chapter. You will remember what it says in verses 6–10: "And he answered and spake unto me, saying, This is the word of the Lord unto Zerubbabel, saying, Not by might, nor by power, but by my Spirit, saith the Lord of hosts. Who art thou, O great mountain? Before Zerubbabel thou shalt become a plain; and he shall bring forth the top stone with shoutings of Grace, grace, unto it. Moreover the word of the Lord came unto me, saying, The hands of Zerubbabel have laid the foundation of this house; his hands shall also finish it; and thou shalt know that the Lord of hosts hath sent me unto you. For who hath despised the day of small things? for these seven shall rejoice and shall see the plummet in the hand of Zerubbabel; these are the eyes of the Lord, which run to and fro through the whole earth."

Our God has given His Word. The mountains of difficulty and problem and impossibility that stand before the building work of

God's Christ will disappear before Him, not by human might or genius, nor by our human activity or endeavour alone, but by His Spirit. Not His Spirit in a vague or ethereal sense, but His Spirit indwelling us as the people of God, anointing us, empowering us, gifting us, and equipping us so that this work of the building can go forward unto completion. His hands began the work. His hands will complete it and the top stone shall be brought forth with shouts of Grace, grace, unto it. God has given us a breathing space. May we take advantage of it and not sleep through these days, not only these days of conference, but these days and years we have of freedom, that we may be enabled to really be in the centre of His will and purpose. "Be not foolish, but understand what the will of the Lord is" (see Ephesians 5:17).

1 Corinthians 12:12–27: "For as the body is one, and hath many members, and all the members of the body, being many, are one body; so also is Christ. For in one Spirit were we all baptized into one body, whether Jews or Greeks, whether bond or free, and were all made to drink of one Spirit. For the body is not one member, but many. If the foot shall say, Because I am not the hand, I am not of the body; it is not therefore not of the body and if the ear shall say, because I am not the eye, I am not of the body; it is not therefore not of the body. If the whole body were an eye, where were the hearing? If the whole were hearing, where were the smelling? But now hath God set the members each one of them in the body, even as it pleased him. If they were all one member, where were the body? But now they are many members, but one body and the eye cannot say to the hand, I have no need of thee: or again the head to the feet, I have no need of you. Nay, much rather, those members of the body which seem to be

more feeble are necessary: and those parts of the body, which we think to be less honourable, upon these we bestow more abundant honour; and our uncomely parts have more abundant comeliness; whereas our comely parts have no need: but God tempered the body together, giving more abundant honour to that part which lacked; that there should be no schism in the body; but that the members should have the same care one for another. And whether one member suffereth, all the members suffer with it; or one member is honoured, all the members rejoice with it. Now ye are the body of Christ, and severally members thereof."

Shall we have a word of prayer? And may every one of us really stand together into that anointing which is ours in the Lord Jesus Christ for speaking and for hearing.

Lord, we bow here in Thy presence and once more we just want to recognize that we are cast upon Thee, utterly dependent upon Thee if Thou art going to get something into our hearts of lasting value. By faith now we all come under the anointing which is ours in the Lord Jesus Christ, that anointing which runs down from the Head to the hem of the garment and covers every single member of the body. By faith we stand into it, speaker and hearer alike, that we may know divine enablement in our speaking and in our hearing, and thus, Lord, may know Thee in this time. We commit ourselves to Thee that Thy will shall be done. In the name of our Lord Jesus Christ. Amen.

I want to read one further verse in 1 Corinthians 1:9: "God is faithful, through whom ye were called into the fellowship of his Son Jesus Christ our Lord." *God is faithful through whom we were called into the fellowship of His Son Jesus Christ our Lord.*

Principle vs. Regulation

It has been my burden to speak about this matter of fellowship and particularly the principles of fellowship. It might be good if we were to define what we mean by principles at the very beginning. A principle is not a regulation. There is a very great difference between regulation and principle. A regulation is something man-made; it comes into human law; but a principle really is in that sphere of natural law.

Let me explain it this way. The speed limit is a regulation; maybe here it is 55 miles per hour. Man has made that, and of course, we are all bound to keep it. Nevertheless, you can drive in an area where it is 55 miles per hour, at 70 miles per hour providing the police do not see you and catch you, providing you do not have an accident, and providing you have no conscience, you can get away with it. There are many, many such speeders, who have done well above the speed limit at different times, and the police have not caught them, they have not had an accident, and they have had little conscience, if any about it. They got away with it. That was a regulation, but they got away with it and nothing happened. If the police did not catch them and they did not have an accident, nothing happened to them.

However, a principle is a very different thing. If you were to go to the top storey of the dormitory that you are sleeping in or the house where you are staying and open the window and step out, the law of gravity will take over. It does not matter whether the whole police force of Ashland is present or not, you will fall with great speed to the ground. It is not a question of whether you are caught or not, the fact is that it is cause and effect. It is a principle.

It is natural law. Something happens the moment you step out of that window. You may have had an hour of prayer, two hours of Bible reading, and a day of fasting, but unless the Lord suspends natural law, you will still fall swiftly to the ground.

That is the difference between regulation and principle. Spiritual law is all principle; it is cause and effect. We are not speaking about regulations of fellowship, as if God has given us a whole lot of things that would be good to keep, particularly if we have a tender conscience towards the Lord, but which we will get away with quite well if we do not keep them, if we break them. We are dealing with principles of fellowship, which mean that if these principles are seen, adhered to and obeyed, then certain consequences will follow. There will be increase. There will be development. There will be cohesion. There will be gifting. There will be equipping, there will be a progress, and there will be authority. All these things flow out of the principles of fellowship. Therefore, you see that it is of the utmost importance that we should understand first what fellowship really is, and secondly how God has called us into it. Then we need to begin to understand some of the principles of true fellowship.

Now what I plan to do, by the grace of God and the enabling of the Holy Spirit, is just to introduce this subject of fellowship. I know that some of you will know as much if not a good deal more than I do on this subject. Nevertheless, it is good for us to look at this whole subject again.

True Fellowship

What is true fellowship? I suppose that fellowship, along with a number of other words, is one of those words which have been devalued by Evangelicals. What is fellowship? Some people seem to think fellowship is friendliness. That is all it is, just a little bit of friendliness. If a few people smile at you, there is a bit of fellowship there. Other people though, say there is no fellowship. Some people seem to think that fellowship is just a kind of *bonhomie*, a kind of comradeship. There is a little bit more there than just friendliness, but that is really all it is.

Others feel that fellowship is informality. If you are in a house meeting, that is fellowship, yet in a chapel, you have no fellowship. The more informal you are, the more unpunctual you are, the more haphazard you are, that is real fellowship. If there is any order, that is bondage and not fellowship. But there is an idea that somehow or other fellowship is informality. There may be some informality, real informality in fellowship. It may be necessary, but nevertheless, that is not what fellowship consists of.

There are others who seem to think that fellowship is chitchat. If you just go and have a little bit of chitchat with one another, a little bit of small talk, that is fellowship. People say, "I am going over to have a spot of fellowship with so and so," and off they go. It is just a little chitchat, a bit of gossip, a few tales retold, perhaps a spiritual word from the calendar thrown in, and that is fellowship. Providing you have had this little bit of chitchat and lifted it up to a higher level than normal, that is fellowship. But that is not fellowship either.

Then, there are others who believe that fellowship is spiritual talk. If you can get a person into a corner and give them a heavy word from Obadiah or a kind of paraphrase of the Sermon on the Mount or an outline of the book of Jonah, or Revelation in three easy lessons, then that is fellowship. But I can tell you this: you can talk for hours on Bible outlines without there being atom of fellowship in it. On the other hand, you can talk about a motorbike together and have deep fellowship in the Lord. It is not just spiritual talk.

There are those, of course, who think fellowship is a meeting. They speak of meeting together as fellowship. You never have fellowship outside of a meeting. When we are meeting together, that is fellowship and not on any other level.

Then again there are those who seem to think that fellowship is a description of an organization or society. We speak of *the* fellowship, *the* fellowship here or *the* fellowship there. Strangely enough, the word is never used like that in the Bible. We never find that it is called *the* fellowship in the sense of the place we go to or the organization to which we belong or a membership of believers to which we are attached as if it is some kind of institution or organization.

Koinonia

Fellowship may include many of these things and may exclude others, but none of these adequately convey the real meaning of the word fellowship. The Greek New Testament word *koinonia* comes from the root "to have in common." It is variously translated in the New Testament. Sometimes it is the word *partner*, sometimes it is the word *partaker*, sometimes it is the word *participate*, and sometimes it is the word *communion*. We have all these words. Fellowship is another word, of course that we have it translated as. I think the best way to understand this word is to use the word *to share, to have in common*. Fellowship is that we all have something in common. We share something and that is the basis and the dynamic of all our fellowship. It is much more fundamental than usually understood.

Listen again to this word: "God is faithful, through whom ye were called into the fellowship of his Son Jesus Christ our Lord." Now let me put it in a free translation: "God is faithful, through whom ye were called into the sharing of his Son Jesus Christ our Lord." Doesn't that transform it? We have this ecclesiastical idea about the fellowship of His Son. Somehow we are so used to the word that it sort of goes in one ear and out of the other. God is faithful through whom ye were called into the sharing of His Son Jesus Christ our Lord.

What is it that we have in common? What do we believe that we have in common? Just think for a moment. Do we have race in common? We certainly do not. There are Asiatics here. There are Occidentals here. There are Jews and there are Gentiles here. We do not have that in common.

Do we have nationality in common? We certainly do not, in spite of the American War of Independence. We have every different nationality under the sun here.

What do we have in common? Maybe we have class in common. Are we all the same class? I don't suppose we are, if we really looked into it. Maybe you have a more level or equal type of class-consciousness on this side, but we do not have it in Europe yet.

What have we got in common? Ah, do we have temperaments in common? No, we have not! There must be every kind of temperament here. Suppose we were the same—our fellowship is that we are all alike. We have the same temperament. We can all shout hallelujah again and again. We are all volatile people. Or perhaps it is the opposite. We are all cautious, quiet people. No, we do not have that in common.

Then what is it that we have in common? Maybe we have denomination in common. We are all Episcopalians or Methodists or good Southern Baptists or any other kind of thing. No, we do not have that either.

Then what is it that we have in common? It is not colour, it is not race, it is not nationalities, it is not class, it is not temperament, and it is not religious denominations. Then what is it that we have in common? We have the Lord Jesus Christ. There is not a person in this place, who is a true believer, who has not come through our Lord Jesus into the family of God. Not one! He is the only way. Jesus said, "I am the door; by Me if any man may enter in He shall be saved." Jesus said, "I am the way, the truth and the life. No man cometh unto the Father but by me." Every single one of us, it does not matter what our colour is, our race, our nationality, our social standing, our temperament, or whatever religious denomination we belong to or have belonged to, the fact of the matter is that we have all come through our Lord Jesus Christ into the salvation of God. We have come to experience a common salvation. It is one salvation that we have. It is not Lutheran salvation, or Episcopalian salvation, or Brethren salvation, or Pentecostal salvation, or Charismatic salvation. It is the salvation of God that we have come into through our Lord Jesus Christ. Now we find that we have something in common. We are all in the one Christ and the one Christ is in all of us. So you begin to understand something of what fellowship is. God is faithful, through whom ye were called into the sharing of his Son Jesus Christ our Lord, into the fellowship of Jesus Christ our Lord. We are all in the one Christ.

How did Paul begin this letter to the Corinthian Church? He says in verse 9: "God is faithful, through whom ye were called into the fellowship of His Son Jesus Christ our Lord." One or two of the modern versions put it: "… into fellowship with His Son Jesus Christ our Lord." I think it is much more accurately rendered "… into the fellowship of His Son Jesus Christ our Lord." But even if we understand it as "… into fellowship with His Son Jesus Christ our Lord" is the Lord that I am having fellowship with different from the Lord you are having fellowship with? Have I got an Episcopalian Christ and you a Lutheran Christ? Have I got a Pentecostal Christ and you a Baptist Christ? Of course not! There is only one Christ, and that one Christ is unique and supreme, absolutely sovereign. God has made Him Head over all things to the church. What a wonderful thing therefore it is when we read through this Corinthian letter and come to the twelfth chapter, and we suddenly find the apostle describing our being together in the one Christ as being members of a body.

One Body, Many Members

> "For as the body is one, and hath many members,
> and all the members of the body, being many, are
> one body; so also is Christ." 1 Corinthians 12:12

There are many, many members and only one body. Christ has within Him as it were, joined to Him many, many members, but there is only one Christ. He comprehends all. He includes all. Every born-again believer is included, and everyone who is religious, but not born again, is excluded.

What a fellowship! My body is a fellowship. I have many members in my body, but they are my fellowship. Ron has his own fellowship. Brother Kaung has his own fellowship. Their fellowships are sitting there on the front row. My toe does not look like my little finger. My ear does not look like my foot. My arm does not look like my thigh, but they are all part of one life, one personality, one intelligence, what there is of it, one being and that is me. This is my fellowship. This is the fellowship of Lance Lambert. My little finger may say, "I belong to the fellowship of Lance Lambert. I am a very small member, but I am in the fellowship of Lance Lambert. I am not in the fellowship of Ron. He has his own little finger and that is in his fellowship. But all these different members, some of which you can see, some of which are inside and hidden, but more important than some of the ones you can see, share one intelligence, one name, one head, one body. Every single part is interdependent and related with the rest. It is a fellowship.

I think that is what the apostle Paul was trying to get at when he said, "God is faithful, through whom ye were called into the fellowship of His Son Jesus Christ our Lord." Have we not devalued the gospel sometimes in the way we have explained it? We seem to have given the impression that all there is to the gospel is that you get saved, you are forgiven, justified, and then we sing hymns, say prayers, and read the Bible. Then one day you go to heaven where we will sit on a cloud and play a harp forever after in a glorified nightie and be a part of an eternal *Hallelujah* chorus. No wonder the world laughs at us: "That kind of thing belongs to the Middle Ages. Is that what their God gave His Son to bring them into, that they would sit on damp clouds, play harps and sing a kind of endless hallelujah? It would be very boring." But that is not the gospel. The gospel that I understand is just as we heard through Stephen Kaung this morning: God has called us and brought us into His Son to be partakers of His divine nature, to be partners in His Son, to become, as it were, members of Christ. I say that is tremendous! No wonder the apostle said, "We are heirs of God and joint heirs with Christ." That is the gospel. God has brought us into fellowship with Himself. God has brought us into the fellowship of Himself, not just some kind of comradeship, not even a friendliness, not even a kind of (if I may put it reverently) spiritual chitchat. God has brought us into the deepest meaning of fellowship. He has made us partakers of His own nature. Through the exceeding great and precious promises, we have become partakers of the divine nature. That is the gospel. What a salvation that I have been brought into such a fellowship!

Union with Christ

Of course, it is true; there is only one salvation. There is only one name by which we are saved, the name of Jesus. There is only one foundation which no one else can lay but which God has laid, Jesus Christ. There is only one life. Jesus said, "I am the life." When you think about it, it is simply wonderful. I am in Christ and you are in Christ, and Christ is in me and Christ is in you.

When you begin to see it like that, a whole lot of things fall into place. It is not taking the Word of God too far, for this is a spiritual entity which God desired from before the foundation of the world. He wanted to bring mankind into such a union with Himself and such a union with one another that He would be in them and they would be in Him. And then the very glory of God would radiate out of them.

What is this idea that some people have got that the glory of God is a kind of spotlight that shines on you? That glory with which our Lord Jesus Christ was transfigured came from within Him and shone out through His flesh and bones and caused even His clothing to be changed. That is the glory of God. You and I were designed for the glory of God. We were meant for the glory of God. It is not that we should become exhibitionists, but that in union with God, He in us and we in Him we should know this divine fellowship. Nor is that fellowship, which God desires, to be something that is an end in itself. There are these little "bless-me groups" that seem to think that the be all and end all of everything is that we should just gather round, shut out the poor dying world all around us and just enjoy ourselves with the Lord. God help us! Our Lord Jesus Christ could have shut out a dying world from the beginning, and not one of us would have been found in the kingdom of God. But He not only enjoyed His Father, He laid down His life for His Father, and in so doing has brought in an enumerable multitude of those who were alienated and divorced from God through sin.

My dear friends, I believe that even when we are finally transfigured in glory, it will be service that we shall delight in. We do not even know what it will mean in the end. We do not even know what it will mean. If you think heaven is going to be some static thing where we all sit around, sort of draping the hall of mansions, sitting around on gilt chairs while angels wait upon us, with various tasty dishes, and then we are all called to sessions of singing, you have another think coming. It is perfectly clear that we shall be caught up in rapturous worship. We shall be taken out of our souls in the worship of the Lord, something that none of us have ever conceived of, so glorious and wonderful will it be. Some of you know it when you have worshipped the Lord with a full heart and there has been that ecstasy of joy that has come into you and just given you a little glimpse of the glory that is yet to be.

But you know, God's genius will never cease. I do not believe God will stop creating things, stop producing things or stop progressing. Never, never, never! I believe that God wants to go on, but this poor old world has come under the blight of sin. We are told that the development of progress which has been arrested will one day be released from the bondage of sin and corruption into all that God originally intended. The wonder of it all is that at the heart of the whole thing is Christ and those who have been brought into the fellowship of His Son by grace. Oh, what a calling that is ours! Don't you think it is just wonderful?!

Brought into the Fellowship of the Son

Let us go back for one moment to this fellowship of His Son and just think again about these matters. We tend to think of fellowship as just a little smile here and there across an aisle, or just an invitation to come and have a cup of coffee, or if you are on a higher level a cup of tea, and so often that is the idea of fellowship. Or sometimes we say to people: "Do come around, and we are going to have a little informal Bible study. It will be nice to have some fellowship, and of course that is fellowship. But it would be entirely to devalue the whole thought of God to say that is all there is to fellowship. The fact of the matter is this: by the grace of God, I, unworthy as I am, insignificant as I am, ugly in sin as I am, God apprehended me and saved me and brought me into His Son, Jesus Christ our Lord. I am continually amazed that the sphere into which God has brought me is His Son, Jesus Christ. It is amazing to me to discover that He is my righteousness. He is my foundation. He is the way by which heaven opens to me. He is, as it were, my clothing. He is my life. In Him are all the treasures of wisdom and knowledge hidden, and in Him I find completeness and fullness. It is all in Him. Isn't it wonderful? It is!

I think I have said this before but I will say it again because I think it helps us to understand. We take a well-known verse such as John 3:16, and we have the whole thing here. "For God so loved the world, that he gave his only begotten Son, that whosoever believeth on him should not perish, but have everlasting life" (ASV). There are very few people who have the King James Version or the Revised Version or the Old Standard Version who ever think about that word "believeth on Him." Have you ever asked yourself why it says, "believeth on Him"? Again, in John 3:36 it says, "He that believeth on the Son hath everlasting life" (ASV). Why does he say "on the Son"? Because the little preposition in Greek is a preposition of motion and literally it means: "God so loved the world that He gave his only begotten Son that whosoever believeth into Him should not perish but have everlasting life." But our godly old translators of the King James Version had much discussion as to how to translate this because it did not seem right in English. Finally, they said, "We cannot translate it "believeth in him" because that means I, here, believe in Him over there, and that is not true. The whole idea is that by my faith I am joined to the Lord, I am carried to the Lord, I am calling on the Lord, I become joined to Him. So they decided on this phrase which you will find nowhere else in English literature, "believeth on him." I do not believe on Harold Wilson, our prime minister. I do not believe on President Ford; I believe in President Ford. I do not believe on the Queen of England; I believe in the Queen of England. But when I am given saving faith by God through the work of His Spirit, then I believe on the Lord Jesus Christ. Something happens which is unique. I am carried into His Son. Through saving faith, God takes me into His Son and joins me to Him so that He who is joined to the Lord is one Spirit. I am in Christ, so Ron also has believed and he is in Christ, and brother Kaung has believed and he is in Christ.

Well, then have we got our own Christ? What is this dreadful term we have in evangelical circles, "a personal Saviour"? As if He is some kind of personal toilet commodity, just like you have your own face flannel or your own toothbrush—your personal toothbrush, your personal face flannel—you have your personal Saviour. But where does it say in the whole New Testament that we have a personal Saviour? We have a personal knowledge of the Saviour, but that is not a personal Saviour. There is not an Episcopalian Saviour, and a Lutheran Saviour, and a Brethren Saviour, and a Pentecostal Saviour, and a Baptist Saviour, and a

Presbyterian Saviour, and a Methodist Saviour. There is only one Saviour and we are all in Him and He is in all of us.

It is even more wonderful that I say that Christ lives in me, and Ron says that is strange because Christ lives in me, and brother Kaung says that is even stranger because He lives in me. If we are all in the same Christ, then the same Christ is in all of us. Now we begin to discover that we have something in common which transcends colour, which transcends race, which transcends nationality, which transcends social standing, which transcends temperament, which transcends all religious denominations. We have our Lord in common. I am in Him; you are in Him. He is in me; He is in you. What has happened to us then may I ask? We must have a relationship one to another. There are some people who say, "You have to be careful of this kind of thing; you are taking it too far." However, if I am in the one Lord and you are in the one Lord and the one Lord is in you and in me, there must be some relationship between us surely. You and I have now got a relationship we never had before, haven't we? Of course, we have. That is why it says in Romans 12:5: "We are one body in Christ." It does not say we are one body of Christ. That is perfectly true and that is how most people read it. But it says, "We are one body in Christ." We are all these members, not only of Christ, but of one another. Do you begin to see how wonderful it really is that God has called us into this fellowship?

Every Child of God Has a Calling

Look again at this word: "God is faithful through whom ye were called into the fellowship of his Son Jesus Christ our Lord."

First of all, consider that word *call*. There is such a lot in the Bible about calling: Walk worthily of your calling. This word *call* comes from the same root as the word church, *ecclesia*, and also coming from the same root word is the word *elect*. We get all these words from the same root—*ecclesia*, the church, the called-out ones. Isn't it strange that we always speak of them as called-out ones because actually ecclesia was an assembly. It was not just called out; it was called. It was a call. They were not only called out of their homes and businesses, but they were to gather together in assembly. "God is faithful through whom ye were called into the fellowship of his Son, Jesus Christ our Lord." Do you know that if you are a child of God you have a calling? This calling is not only that you have been called out of the world, called out of sin, called out of darkness, but you have been called into the fellowship of His Son. You have been called into Christ, and you have been called into the sharing of His Son.

I also think it is very wonderful when we think about it that from the very beginning God has desired this fellowship. It is in the very nature of God to want to include us. It is amazing, isn't it? Really when you think about it, we are worthless. We are little bits of worthless clay into which God has breathed an eternal spirit and produced a living soul. When you think of it, God has gone to such lengths! When we fell, when we turned away, God did not give us up. God has called us back into His original purpose that you and I could be partakers of the divine nature and we should become His heirs and joint heirs with Christ.

I find it a very wonderful thought that God uses here the word faithful. "God is faithful through whom you were called into the fellowship of His Son, Jesus Christ our Lord." Only those of us who have seen something of this and have committed our lives lock, stock, and barrel to it will discover that all hell comes out against any such thing as real fellowship. Satan seems to have a vested interest in destroying fellowship just because it means so much to God.

Every Member Has a Part

When we consider this Corinthian letter, what a breakdown of fellowship there was. There were all kinds of things in this church which were a denial of fellowship, a contravening of all the principles of fellowship. Right at the beginning the apostle said, "God is faithful through whom ye were called into the fellowship of his Son, Jesus Christ our Lord." Every single member is vital in this fellowship. My little finger may not seem very much to me, but it has a part to play somewhere in my whole body. Every single member has a part to play. Every member is necessary. I often think when we go to some places that we could write over them the word in 1 Corinthians 12:19: "And if they were all one member, where were the body?" Because today in many places it is all one member. Generally speaking, the pastor starts the meeting, leads the meeting, gives out the hymn, says the prayers, gives the Bible reading, gives another hymn, but generally allows someone else to give out the notices and take up the collection. Then he gives out another hymn, then preaches the word, then prays, then gives out another hymn, and finally gives the benediction. Really you could write over it: "If the body were one member, where were the body?"

This fellowship is something so wonderful! Every one of us is not only a king and a priest, but we can come and offer sacrifices to God. We are meant to do that together. I am only seeking to introduce in this whole matter of fellowship. Later, we shall take up some of these things and talk about some of the specific principles. However, it is a strange thing that all the historic fellowships and Protestant denominations have believed in the priesthood of all believers. Yet hardly any of them, with a few notable exceptions, have ever given place for the exercise of that principle.

Fellowship is not that all the members do the same thing, but there are many members with different functions. They are all interrelated and in one sense interdependent, and the full increase and growth of the whole is dependent upon the way each part of the body functions. You all know what happens when some small muscle gives up. You get, what we call in England, neuralgia or sciatica. Suddenly someone says, "Ow! It is only the smallest muscle, but such pain!" You know what it is sometimes to put out a finger. You would think that the pain and discomfort is out of all proportion to the silly little member that has been put out. If it does not paralyze completely, it makes the functioning of the whole body a matter of difficulty.

Isn't it a wonderful thing when our whole body is healthy? For those of you who are blessed with good health you never think about your body. You can get up out of a chair and get back into a chair; you can lie down on a bed and never think once about it until something goes wrong. Suddenly, the simplest things in life that you have never thought about become really difficult. It is the same with other things as well. But it is all a question of fellowship, isn't it? When our body is a healthy fellowship, we do not even have to think about it because we can get on with the job. We grow, we develop, and our ministry in life is fulfilled.

The Work of the Holy Spirit and Fellowship

I would like to just say something about the work of the Holy Spirit and fellowship. In II Corinthians 13:14 it says: "The grace of the Lord Jesus Christ, and the love of God, and the fellowship of the Holy Spirit, be with you all." The communion or the fellowship of the Holy Spirit. The only way we came into Christ is by new birth. That was the way we came into the body of our Lord Jesus Christ and that is the way we come into this fellowship of His Son, by the Holy Spirit. It is as we were born of the Spirit that we were born into the fellowship of God's Son. Nevertheless, we must say this, we will never function, we will never contribute, we will never grow up together, and we will never be built together apart from the Holy Spirit. It is not enough to say that we had an experience of the Holy Spirit at conversion and that there is no more to be had. The fact of the matter is that there is an anointing of the Holy Spirit. There is a fullness of the Holy Spirit. There are the gifts of the Holy Spirit. There is the equipping by the Holy Spirit. There can be no functioning of fellowship until the Holy Spirit is free. However, when the Holy Spirit is free, the thing becomes a spontaneous reality.

It is a tragedy sometimes when we go to groups who know all about the church. They have got all the doctrines quite clear, but there seems to be no functioning of fellowship. There seems to be no ministry of one member to the other; there does not seem to be any idea of being built together or any sharing of the Lord together. I have discovered, whatever people may think about the Holy Spirit and His work, for and against, that wherever the Holy Spirit has touched people, touched a company, or touched individuals, you begin to find that they move into fellowship.

Of course, we know that there are excesses and we know there are extremes, but how can we really know this fellowship of His Son, Jesus Christ our Lord in practice, in actual reality, apart from the Holy Spirit? It is the Holy Spirit who empowers us and the Holy Spirit who becomes the dynamic.

The Church was Birthed

In the book of Acts we find a remarkable thing. There were one hundred and twenty saved people in an upper room gathered around the risen Lord with a Bible opened up to them by the risen Christ. There could have been no more perfect congregation in the whole world. I know that there are many, many people who would be thrilled to the marrow if every so-called church in the United States consisted of truly born-again believers gathered around a risen Christ with an open Bible and pure doctrine. These one hundred and twenty people gathered in an upper room had no question about the resurrection of Jesus Christ; He was in their midst. There was no question about the Bible and its authority and inspiration for he Himself had opened it up. By the way, there was only the Old Testament; there was no New Testament then. From Genesis right the way through the

Chronicles in the Jewish arrangement, including every book of the Old Testament, they believed in its authority and inspiration because He had opened it up and given them an understanding of the Scriptures. They believed in His virgin birth. They believed in His miraculous ministry. They believed in His atoning death. They believed in His bodily resurrection. They believed in His ascension, and they believed He would come back in the same way by which He was taken from them. But our Lord appears to be afraid that those hundred and twenty would begin going all over the place starting congregations of such believers. He said to them: "Wait in Jerusalem until the Holy Spirit comes upon you and you shall be witnesses unto Me in Jerusalem, in Judea, in Samaria, and to the uttermost parts of the earth" (Acts 1:8). When the Holy Spirit came, it was one Spirit that came, and suddenly there were one hundred and twenty cloven tongues of fire that settled upon one hundred and twenty units in a congregation. Then the miracle took place. The one hundred and twenty units became one hundred and twenty members of a body. It was an essential difference that took place. There was no more casting of lots to find out who should take the place of Judas. From then on they sought the Lord with prayer and fasting and found the mind of God through the Spirit of God. From then on it was the Spirit of God who said, "Separate Paul and Barnabas." From then on there was no more rivalry, no more infighting in that sense, although they had their problems and collisions.

You remember when Peter stood up to preach on that day of Pentecost, the eleven stood up with him. They did not open their mouths to begin with to preach that message. Yet no one said, "Who does he think he is? Why doesn't he sit down and let me have a go?" It was as if the whole eleven thought: "He is our mouth. What he is saying, we are saying. He is our mouth. We cannot explain it. We are so together with him, we are such a part of him that what he is saying, we are saying. We are right in it."

Peter and John saw a man who was a paralytic. They acted together, but it was Peter who spoke, and said, "Silver and gold have I none, but such as I have give I unto Thee. Rise up in the name of Jesus of Nazareth" (Acts 3:6). The fact of the matter is that John did not have a bad time because Peter said I. "Peter is speaking for me. We are in this thing together."

We must never be afraid of the Holy Spirit. I do not know any single occasion in the history of the church that the Holy Spirit has started to move where there has not been excess or extreme. There will always be excess and extreme. The enemy will work unceasingly to bring in trouble, wrong teaching, factions, self-seeking, divisions and so on, but the fact remains that what is right is right. We need the Holy Spirit. "The grace of our Lord Jesus Christ and the love of God and the fellowship of the Holy Spirit be with you all" (ii Corinthians 13:14). We need the Holy Spirit to release us in fellowship, to release all the gifts of Christ among us, to bring out the beauties of Christ, to bring out the excellencies of Christ, to enable us to overcome fear and bondage and all the inhibitions that hold us back from really functioning in the body of our Lord Jesus Christ.

The Consequences of True Fellowship

The second thing I would like to say in closing is this: there are some glorious consequences of the reality of true fellowship. When the Holy Spirit begins to make this fellowship of God's Son, Jesus Christ our Lord a living reality amongst the people of God, some marvellous things begin to happen.

An Expression of Christ

First of all, I believe there is an expression of Christ. What do we mean by an expression of Christ? "One thing have I desired of the Lord, that will I seek after: that I may dwell in the house of the Lord all the days of my life, to behold the beauty of the Lord" (Psalm 27:4). I believe this poor world longs to see something of the Lord Jesus. All it sees are our meetings, our talk, our doctrine, our preaching, and our activities. If only the world could see Jesus! If only the world could see the beauty of the Lord Jesus! If only the world could see the power of the Lord Jesus! If only the world could see the character of the Lord Jesus!

The Lord Jesus can never fully express Himself through one Christian, not even through two Christians, three Christians, four Christians. He needs us all through whom to express something of His fullness and glory. What a wonderful thing it is when we are sharing Him, when we are really related to one another in Him, when we are moving together in and with Him! Then somehow the beauty of the Lord our God is upon us. There are failings, there are faults, there are collisions, there are shortcomings, and we all know them. However, the Lord covers them with His beauty, and people coming in amongst us touch the

Lord and see the Lord. We are very conscious of the work that is being done inside—the cutting work, the shaping work, the fitting work, the knitting of us together. When people come in, they are not conscious of any tension, or strain, or problems, but they only see the Lord. What a wonderful thing it is when unsaved people come to you and say, "There is something about this company. I have never seen it before."

I have known atheists come to me, and they will not even say it is God. I remember one man who came week after week after week to the company in Richmond, England. He was an atheist and said to me, "I have been in Bahá'í temples, Hindu temples, mosques, and synagogues. I have been in everything, but there is something about this people here that I cannot explain. Sometimes he said it with tears in his eyes. He never found the Lord, not yet anyway. But even an atheist had to confess that there was something more than people. Oh, if only in Washington, in Richmond, in New York, and all the many other places we came from there were such a fellowship amongst the people of God, such a sharing of the Lord that Christ expressed. It is not only that unsaved people need to see the Lord; many Christians need to see the Lord. There are many casualties amongst the people of God, many people who are down cast and do not know where to turn. All they see everywhere is what is wrong. Oh, that they could see the Lord!

Authority

There is something else that I would like to mention which is a result of true fellowship, and that is authority. You can have your deliverance ministries, but unless they are related to the church all of them will ultimately fail. I do not know of a single deliverance ministry that has not gone off the rails in the end unless it is church centred. That is, it knows something of the meaning of fellowship and authority. God longs above everything else that His people here on earth should be the means by which His authority is established over localities, over areas. We are wrestling not against flesh and blood, but against principalities, against powers, against the world rulers of this darkness, against hosts of wicked spirits in heavenly places.

There is a sense in which what God wants to do with us is to so build us together that the authority of the Lord Jesus Christ might be manifested in our communities, that somehow or other the will of God should be done in the areas in which we live. We are so helpless. Do you know that some companies of Christians do not even know what is happening in their areas? The pornographic filth can sweep over the city and does not seem to bother them. The Lord Jesus said, "You are the salt of the earth," but it does not seem to bother them. All they are concerned about is growing in the Lord. They do not seem to think that it is their concern that they should stand there spiritually, and in the end seize and crush in the name of the risen Christ those powers of darkness and paralyze them. It can be done! It must be done! It is the job of the church to take the enemies of the Lord Jesus Christ and put them under His feet where they belong. But if you and I do not do it, God will not.

The Lord Jesus said, "Upon this rock I will build my church and the gates of hell shall not prevail against it," (Matthew 16:18b) but we have to say the gates of hell have prevailed against it again and again and again. Why? Why? Because the Lord went on to say, "To thee have I given the keys of the kingdom of heaven and whatsoever thou shalt bind on earth shall be bound in heaven, and whatsoever thou shalt loose on earth shall be loosed in heaven" (Matthew 16:19). What our Lord wants are companies of His people so built together, whose lives have been laid down for Christ's sake and for one another that the authority of the risen Christ can be manifested in the areas in which we live. It is not right, dear child of God, for us just to say the Bible says things are going to get worse and worse and worse until we fall in the ground, as it were, and say, "All right then, so let it be." Our job is to maintain things for God and to see that the enemies of our Lord Jesus Christ do not overcome the work of God and do not destroy the building work of Christ.

Now let me say this. If there are evil things in your area, whether you know it or not, they are affecting the building of the church in your area. For all these things are spiritual entities and until they have been dislodged and paralyzed and bound there is no way for the work to go forward. What did our Lord Jesus say? If you want to spoil the strong man and take his goods, first you must bind him. Woe betide any believer who thinks he can exercise the authority of the Lord Jesus Christ outside of fellowship. Woe betide any agency, of deliverance or anything else, that thinks it can exercise the authority of our Lord Jesus in that whole realm of principalities, and powers, and world rulers of darkness, and hosts of wicked spirits outside of fellowship. These are church matters. These are things that belong to the realm of the body of the Lord Jesus Christ. They belong to that realm of fellowship where we are hidden in Him.

The Presence of the Lord

Lastly, another result of fellowship is that the presence of the Lord is found on earth. In 1 Corinthians 14:25, the apostle said that a man shall come in and fall down and worship, saying, "God is here." Beyond all our preaching, beyond all our meetings, beyond all our presentation of doctrines, the most glorious thing of all is the presence of the Lord. When the presence of the Lord has gone, the rest is so much paraphernalia. But when the presence of the Lord is there, things happen. God commits Himself, when He finds a people who know something of the fellowship of His Son in their experience. It is the presence of the Lord. I do not think that the United States could have anything more wonderful or more glorious than that in every company represented here in this place tonight, it could be said, "The presence of the Lord is committed here." When they gather, they gather unto the Lord. When they are found together, it is the Lord who manifests Himself through them. It is His presence that makes a lasting impression upon all who come in. Oh, may the Lord do it! "God is faithful through whom ye were called into the fellowship of his Son, Jesus Christ our Lord."

Shall we pray?

Dear Lord, we lift up our hearts together to Thee. Thou knowest our needs, Lord. Oh, we pray that Thou would not allow any of what has been said just, as it were, to be dissipated. We pray, beloved Lord that Thou would cause what is Thy Word to dwell in us richly. Oh Father, block out anything untoward or anything that has been said which has been imbalanced or wrong. But Lord, everything which is of Thyself, watch over it to perform it. Oh, we pray that we Thy people will be those who may know something of this fellowship in reality and practice. We ask, Lord, that Thou will work out all the individualism and all those areas of resistance and rebellion. Oh Father, by Thy Spirit work in us all we pray, so that we not only see what fellowship is but we will commit ourselves to Thee in a new way. May we know that blessed fellowship of Thy Spirit. Oh Father, we commit ourselves to Thee. In the name of Thy dear Son, our Lord Jesus Christ. Amen.

2.
The Unity of Fellowship

John 17:20–26

Neither for these only do I pray, but for them also that believe on me through their word; that they may all be one; even as thou, Father, art in me, and I in thee, that they also may be in us: that the world may believe that thou didst send me. And the glory which thou hast given me I have given unto them; that they may be one, even as we are one; I in them, and thou in me; that they may be perfected into one; that the world may know that thou didst send me, and lovedst them, even as thou lovedst me. Father, I desire that they also whom thou hast given me be with me where I am, that they may behold my glory, which thou hast given me: for thou lovedst me before the foundation of the world. O righteous Father, the world knew thee not, but I knew thee; and these knew that thou didst send me; and I made known unto them thy name, and will make it known; that the love wherewith thou lovedst me may be in them, and I in them.

Ephesians 4:1–3

I therefore, the prisoner in the Lord, beseech you to walk worthily of the calling wherewith ye were called, with all lowliness and meekness, with longsuffering, forbearing one another in love; giving diligence to keep the unity of the Spirit in the bond of peace.

Psalm 133:1–3

Behold, how good and how pleasant it is for brethren to dwell together in unity! It is like the precious oil upon the head, that ran down upon the beard, even Aaron's beard; that came down upon the skirt of his garments; like the dew of Hermon, that cometh down upon the mountains of Zion: for there the Lord commanded the blessing, even life for evermore.

Shall we pray?

Father, we do thank Thee that we are gathered here in Thy presence, and we want to recognise and confess that Thou hast made our Lord Jesus Christ Head over all things to the church. We thank Thee, Father, that Thou hast made Him our Lord and our Head, and we recognise His headship. We look to Thee that we might know the most wonderful ministry of Thy Spirit to our hearts, things that perhaps we already know and they come to us with fresh life and power, and things that we have not seen before we may see. Where there is only a mental or academic appreciation of these things, oh Father, grant to us that Spirit of wisdom and revelation in the knowledge of Thyself that the eyes of our heart being enlightened we might know these things.

Lord, we do thank Thee that there is this anointing upon the head that runs down to the very hem of the garment. We thank Thee for the anointing upon the head, our Lord Jesus that runs down to include every member of the body, and together now we all stand into it. Whether in hearing or speaking, we all confess our bankruptcy when it comes to spiritual things. But Lord, we praise Thee that Thou hast made provision for us, and we would come through the righteousness of Thy Son on the basis of His finished work, and we would take the provision that we need for this morning. We stand into the anointing for every single member of the body here for speaker and for hearer alike that we might know Thy presence in our midst and hear Thy voice beyond the human word and hear what the Spirit says to us. We do ask it, Father, with thanksgiving. In the name of our Lord Jesus Christ. Amen.

1 Corinthians 1:9: "God is faithful, through whom ye were called into the fellowship of His Son Jesus Christ our Lord." I have already introduced this matter of fellowship and we have seen that real fellowship is not just a little bit of friendliness or informality or spiritual talk or just meeting together, but it is that we share something special together. We have something in common, and of course, it is our Lord Jesus Christ. "God is faithful, through whom you were called into the sharing of His Son Jesus Christ our Lord." I am in the Son and you are in the Son; the Son is in you and the Son is in me. I have something to give of the Son that you do not have to give and you have something to give of the Son that I do not have to give. Therefore, as we share the Son we come into a fullness, we come into an understanding, we grow in grace, and we grow up into Him as the Head.

Of course, this basic sharing of the Lord Jesus Christ naturally affects every other thing—our time, our home, our possessions, our energy. All of it is shared. It does not mean that you allow your things to be abused or misused. There is this idea that once you see that everything you have belongs to the Lord and it is therefore at the disposal of the church, that somehow or other people can just come in and do what they like. You must stand by and just watch them spoil your home or spoil your car. I know people, for instance, who feel they must let their car out to anybody, and there are some people who come along and cannot drive the for toffey. Because they feel that their car is no longer their own, it is the Lord's, they should allow someone who cannot drive to drive it. The person thinks he can drive because he has a license, but the way he drives is anybody's business. So while we are not the owners of what we possess, we are the stewards, and we are responsible to God for all that belongs to Him. In other words, even though our homes are His and at the disposal of the family of God, we are stewards of them. We are not to let just any Tom, Dick, or Harry take over. We are not permitted just to allow anyone to take our things and spoil them or misuse them. We are stewards. We are responsible to the Head. We are responsible to the Lord Jesus to give an answer for the way these possessions of ours are used. This is a very important point to make.

The Oneness of Christ

I want to talk now about one of those principles of fellowship, which is fundamental and essential for this whole matter. The first principle of fellowship is the principle of unity. I do not think there is any principle related to this matter of fellowship that is more important than the principle of unity. The unity of God's people is not just some luxury to be desired, but we can do without it. It is not just some kind of regulation that we can break with impunity if there is no one there to see us break it or we do not have some accident as it were. This is a principle. If we contravene the principle of the oneness of Christ then the consequences are always the same and always follow. There is no stopping them. Once we contravene or contradict the principle of the oneness of Christ, then death results. Paralysis results. Weakness results. Heaviness results. Bondage results. Corporate inhibition results—there is a kind of tension and strain about everything. But once we recognise and obey the principle of the oneness of Christ, then immediately we discover that there is development, there is increase, there is expression of Christ, there is the equipping of the saints, there is the raising up in our midst of ministries, and there is the qualifying of leadership. All these things result from the principle of the oneness of Christ being recognised and obeyed. Therefore, there is no principle more important than this.

I go around to many companies in different places, and I see in many of the companies those who recognise a certain amount of church truth. They see something of the nature of the church. They see something of the ministries of the church. They see something of the purpose of God. Yet their great cry is: Why is there no real leadership? Why are there no real ministries amongst us? Why are there not being raised up in our midst men who have the ministry of God's Word—prophets, teachers, evangelists? It always goes back to this point that somewhere or other some essential and fundamental principle of fellowship is being contradicted. Here is one of them.

What is the basis of our fellowship together? It is a good question. What is the basic of our fellowship together? Listen carefully to this because even though we say the basis of our fellowship is Christ, we can deceive ourselves. Although we say it is Christ, in practice it may be many other things. What is the basis upon which alone we can know true fellowship? It is not truth, however important. It is not teachings, however correct. It is not experiences, however necessary. It is not emphases of truth, or technique, or our denominations, or the membership roll. Oh, there are many things that we make the basis of our fellowship!

First and Second Class Citizens

For instance, some groups will make baptism in water the rule of membership. You are allowed to attend, but until you have been baptized by immersion, you are not in the church; you are not a member of the church. Others make some other point, for instance, some experience of the Holy Spirit the sort of key to being let in. There are many groups who will say, "No, we do not expect that." Nevertheless, there are first and second-class citizens. There are those who have seen and those who have not seen, and those who have seen are in, and those who have not seen are out. Those who have not seen are made to feel very out by those who are in and who have seen. In other words, the line all along is: you have got to see, you have got to see, you have got to see. We do not leave it to the Holy Spirit to draw people into our fellowship because we all love Christ and because we include every single one who is in Christ. Oh, no, no, no! We are all the time labouring the point that there is something this person has not experienced, something this person has not seen. Therefore we make of our fellowship a first and second-class citizenship. There are those who are first-class citizens. They are the ones who have seen or experienced and are in the elite inner circle; and there are those who have not seen, and they are outside.

Now, do not get me wrong on this matter. Of course there are things we have to see in a living church, in the church as God would have it, which would include every believer of all shapes, sizes, sorts, and colours. The fact of the matter is that there will always be those who have not seen and there will always be those who have seen, and who are progressively seeing more of the Lord. But every single thing depends upon the attitude of those who have seen. It is not those who have not seen who are the problem; it is the people who have seen who are the problem. It is not those who have not had experiences that are the problem; it is those who have had the experiences who are the problem.

Sometimes the Lord may take years with us to bring us to a place where we see something, but the moment we see it we expect others immediately, in an instant to come in. We will give them tracts, pamphlets, books, send them postal courses of instruction and I don't know what else to get them in as quickly as possible. The impression we give is that we are in and they are out. We love them. Why do we give them the pamphlets? Why do we give them the tracts? It is not just because, as in some cases, we are looking upon them as more people to be counted. It is that in many cases we have a real love and concern for the people of God, but our whole conception of fellowship is wrong. Babies are babies. You do not put babies in a high school. You care for babies until they grow to such an age that they can go through the various stages of education and enter high school and finally university. Whatever is wrong with our fellowship that all the time we expect that as soon as a person is born again they must somehow grow in some kind of greenhouse soooo swiftly, in a manner of moments, to see all that we have seen? Such understanding is nearly always artificial and false.

Spiritual Things are Organic

I believe that when in any company of God's people there is a nucleus of those who have really seen and really experienced things of the Lord and are going deeper with Him and are laying down their lives for the whole, then it is true that those who are saved will rapidly grow. They will not need to go through the years that we went through.

I remember I went through four years of darkness before I came into an experience of the Holy Spirit and of the cross. I promised the Lord when I came to that place that I would give to every person who ever found the Lord through me by His grace, a full gospel, the whole counsel of God and not just a little bit that I had to live on. Nevertheless, we must understand that spiritual things are organic. They cannot be organized. Don't you see that we who have believed so much in the organic nature of everything that is spiritual are ourselves guilty of organizing things? We are always organizing everything so that those who smoke will not smoke, and those who drink will not drink, and those who are worldly will not be worldly, and those who have not had an experience of holiness will immediately have an experience of holiness, and those who have not had a baptism in the Spirit will have a baptism in the Spirit. We are organizing everything all the time. We do not leave it to the organic.

The Basis of Our Fellowship

What is the basis of our fellowship? Now there must be a minimum truth. That is obvious. We must be very careful that we do not go too far in this matter, as if when we say, "Truth is not the basis of our fellowship, but Christ," we give the impression that it is some ethereal, abstract, vague Christ. Christ is the truth and there is a sense in which there is minimal truth concerning the Person of God, concerning the Person of our Lord Jesus Christ, concerning His atoning death and His bodily resurrection. These things are essential truths. No one can really be in the fellowship who does not at least recognise them. They may not understand it all, but that is minimum. However, beyond that there are a thousand and one other truths.

I know companies where people have been put out because they believe that we are going to go through the tribulation. My goodness me! Do you put people out of fellowship because they believe we are going to go through the tribulation? I wish I could be as dogmatic as that. So we are all going to be raptured before the tribulation, are we? There are other groups that look down their noses at anyone who believes we are going to be raptured before the tribulation. Then there are those blessed and most spiritual of all people who believe that we shall be taken during the tribulation. Then only those who are ready for the Lord shall be taken. Shall we divide on such things?

I know of an assembly in a place in Britain called Totterdown, and they put out a dear brother who I know very well simply because he believed that only the overcomer would be raptured. He did not divide the saints; he did not even major on it. He just happened to believe it, so they put him out. Of course, they lived up to their name; they "tottered down."

You cannot put out someone whom God has received on some basis like that. The whole danger of the Charismatics (and I speak from some experience with the Charismatics) is that we make the charismatic the basis for fellowship. Thank God for everyone who has been renewed by the Spirit of God. People tell me that the Charismatic is all up the wall, and full of extremes, and excesses, but I tell you that I know literally thousands of people who were dead, dry bones before the Spirit of God came upon them. Am I to deny that the Spirit of God has come upon them? Suddenly I find them full of spiritual life, full of the Lord, full of Christ. Suddenly those who were static are moving on with God. I cannot deny that God has done something. From my heart I thank God for all that He has done through the Charismatics, but to make the charismatic the basis of fellowship or even to make a first and second-class citizenship is utterly wrong.

Of course, it hardly needs to be said here that there are those who meet on the ground of denominationalism. There are those who meet on the ground of Christ plus Methodism, and others who meet on the ground of Christ plus baptism. Others meet on the ground of Christ plus Episcopalianism, and others who meet on the ground of Christ plus Pentecostalism. But this is not the basis of our fellowship.

Christ Alone

What is the basis of our fellowship? It is Christ alone, not Christ plus, nor Christ minus, not less than Christ, nor more than Christ. The foundation of our fellowship, the basis of our fellowship is Christ. We must receive all on this basis. We cannot reject one whom Christ has received, for it says in Romans 15:7: "Wherefore receive ye one another even as Christ also received you to the glory of God." How did Christ receive me? Did He receive me as an elite going-on saint? No. Did He receive me as someone who would be a servant of the Lord? No. Did He receive me as someone who would please Him? No. Did He receive me as someone who was ready to go through the waters of baptism? No. Did He receive me as someone who was prepared to know an experience of the cross? No. How did He receive me? He received me as a hopeless sinner whom He saved by His grace through the work of the Lord Jesus Christ. That was the basis upon which He received me.

How shall I receive you? If I were to receive you on the minimum basis that you are a sinner saved by grace, all my problems would be over. But we do not receive one another as sinners saved by grace. We receive one another as great saints. We see those lovely shining faces and we say, "Oh, it is lovely being with so and so; he or she is such a saint,"—until we get to know them. Then, suddenly we find the spiritual cosmetics disappear. The spiritual hairdos go. We see them, as it were, in their bedroom, spiritually. We see them with their hair down or their hair in curlers or their teeth out, and suddenly we are shocked to the marrow. "Oh," we think, "dear, dear, I never thought it of so and so. I thought so and so was so spiritual, but I can't have fellowship anymore with so and so. It is no good; it is no good. My fellowship with so and so is ruined. You poor soul." Is that the basis of your fellowship? Is that the basis of your fellowship? So you reject someone whom Christ has received.

We have this weird idea that God is always getting surprises about us. It is a strange thing that we all have this idea that God took us on and was quite pleased with us after He saved us, and then He begins to find out things about us. We lose our temper, and then we feel that God is so disillusioned. Then the devil comes and says, "Now don't you pray again. It is no good praying because God is so upset." Or maybe you get irritated or some unclean thought comes into your head, and in that moment the devil comes to you and says, "Now you cannot pray; God is so disillusioned with you. He is disappointed with you."

But do you know that when God saved you, He has your whole life like an open book? He saw every single thing that you would ever do as it were already an open book. I am a good Calvinist in this matter. God saw every single thing about you when He saved you; there is not a thing about you that will surprise Him. Do you know that He still saved you? He still saved you with all that rebellion in the future, with all that resistance that He saw, with all that ugliness, with all that sort of refusal to allow Him to deal with you. Still He saved you with your whole life as an open book before Him. God is not surprised. You are the one who is surprised. Do you know what it is that stops us from coming back to Him? It is our pride. You see, often we get so surprised about ourselves, so shocked that because we are shocked about ourselves, we think God is. God does not condone our sins, but He is not surprised. God knows our capacity for evil far, far more fully than we do. He knows what we are capable of if we are subjected to the right temptation. That is why He taught us to pray: "Lead us not into temptation but deliver us from the evil one."

My point is this: God is quite "unshockable" when it comes to you. He knows everything about you and a good deal more than you know about yourself. He knows what you are capable of and still He receives you as a sinner whom He saved. Now, you and I are to receive one another as Christ also received us. He received me as a sinner. Now I must receive you as a sinner. Well, we are going to get down to brass tacks now. That means I have got to receive you with your spiritual teeth out. I have got to receive you for what you are. The fact is this: If God has received you through Christ, I must receive you. Can I reject someone whom Christ has received?

People tell me again and again in my fellowship with Catholics that I should have nothing to do with them, that I am being deluded and deceived, and I don't know what else. But can I reject someone who happens to be a Roman Catholic whom God has received? Never! Am I to receive some dead nominal Lutheran as a brother whom God has not received through Jesus Christ, but to reject the Roman Catholic whom God has received through Jesus Christ? I cannot do it. If God has received a person I must receive that person. If God has received that one on the basis of His finished work, I receive that one on the basis of His finished work.

If you whittle down your fellowship to one less than the Father has received, you will contradict the principle of the oneness of Christ. Put them out by any other reason than for apostasy or discipline and you have put out Christ.

Unity in Ephesians 4

I want you to notice that there are two kinds of unity in Ephesians 4. In verse 3 we have the unity of the Spirit. Will you notice how we are introduced to it? "Giving diligence to keep the unity of the Spirit in the bond of peace." Then notice in verse 13: "Till we all attain unto the unity of the faith, and of the knowledge of the Son of God, unto a full-grown man." Do you notice there are two kinds of unity here? First, we have the unity of the Spirit, and we are told that we are to keep or to maintain the unity of the Spirit. Then we have the unity of the faith and of the knowledge of the Son of God to which we are to attain. We in Christian circles have inverted the order. We have made the unity of the faith something that is the basis for our fellowship and the unity of the Spirit something we are coming to.

The Unity of the Spirit

God says the unity of the Spirit is something which is yours and you entered it by new birth. When you were born of God, you were born into the unity of the Spirit. You were born into the oneness of Christ. Did you notice those wonderful words of our Lord Jesus Christ "that they may all be one even as Thou Father art in Me and I in Thee that they may be in us"? (John 17:21). Do you realise that this unity, which is ours, is the same inexplicable unity that exists between the Father and the Son and which has never at any time been adequately reduced to human words? "Father, I am in Thee and Thou art in Me that they may be in Us." Now you begin to understand something of this idea brother Stephen Kaung spoke about of the counsel of God. Here you really see the desire of God to bring us into Himself, to bring us into a union with Himself, to make us partakers of His own nature and in so doing make us, as it were, one body—"that they may be in Us."

Now you understand the principle of unity. If we contradict the principle of unity we do damage to the very nature of God. In some way, it is not just the nature of the church, but also the very nature of the trinity. In some way we sin against it when we are part of a faction or a division.

If I were to go and get drunk, I believe you would be shocked. You would say straightaway: "What a dreadful thing! They asked that brother to come and speak to us and he got drunk. What kind of people are they who organized this time that they asked a brother to come to us who has such a feeling for drink?" But if I got drunk (and I am not in any way lessening the sin), the fact of the matter is that I have sinned against my own body. However, it is an extraordinary thing that we can all be part of divisions or factions or out of sorts with one another, and no one sees it as a sin against the body of Christ. If I commit immorality I have sinned, but I have sinned against my own body, and against my own being. But when I am a part of a faction or a division or I am in a state of collision with another saint, I am sinning against the body of our Lord Jesus.

Those very solemn words were said about those who do not discern the body of our Lord, not meaning the bread and wine, but the spiritual entity that is contained and expressed in the bread and the wine. It says, "For this cause some are weak, some are sick, and some have died." That is what this principle of unity means. It is cause and effect. There are sicknesses among the people of God that are due wholly to the fact that people are in a state of division. There is weakness among the people of God wholly due to the fact that we are in a state of division. There are even deaths. Now don't argue with me about this; it is in the Word in I Corinthians 11:27–30. But, we begin to realise the serious nature of this whole matter of oneness when we begin to see that the unity that exists between us and our Lord and between ourselves is the same essential unity as between the Father and the Son. It is something that God has brought us into—one life, eternal life, the life of God; it is one life.

Having said that, I want to say something more on this matter so that we can get ourselves even clearer here. We have a unity of the Spirit, and we are told in Ephesians 4:3 "give diligence to keep the unity." It is ours; we have been born into it. Thank God! Are you a child of God? You have been born into this oneness. You do not have to fight toward it; you do not have to somehow attain to it. You do not have to make it your goal; it is yours. You may be the youngest Christian in the place, but you have been born into this oneness. By the grace of God you have been introduced to the oneness of Christ. You are experiencing it even if you do not know it. That is why every young believer who is first saved, before the older believers get their clammy hands on them, the first thing they feel is a wonderful love toward all the people of God. I have never known a single person who is first saved say that he was a Baptist, or a Methodist, or an Episcopalian, or any of the other multitudinous denominations you have on this side of the Atlantic. I have only found that when a person is saved they are full of love for the people of God. It is when the rest of the older believers start to get their sticky hands on them and sort of say, "Now you are a Baptist. You are a Methodist. You must understand you have been saved into the correct people, the proper people, the only people."

Unity of the Faith

However, there is a unity of the faith which we are to come to, that we are to arrive at. It says, "Until we all attain unto the unity of the faith and of the knowledge of the Son of God," Ephesians 4:13. This unity that is ours is a fact, but we have to be perfected into one. Notice in John 17 our Lord first says in verse 21, "That they may all be one even as Thou Father art in Me and I in Thee that they also be in us." Then in verse 23 He says, "I in them, and thou in me, that they may be perfected into one." In other words, first we have something which is a *fait accompli*, something done, something which is already ours; it is a fact. But the second thing is that when we are in it we then have to be perfected into it. We are to grow up into the Head; we are to be knit together; we are to be fitly framed together. We have to find each other in the Lord. We have to work at it.

This unity of the Spirit is not something you can just say, "Oh yes, yes, of course, we are all one. Christ is our oneness. Good-bye," and you are off; you live your own sweet little life, contained within your own family circle. You come to meetings, you see the saints, you sing a few hymns, say a few prayers, listen to a word or two, you participate if you have a freer type of meetings, and off you go. That is all there is. Somehow or other you feel that somewhere in the great unseen this fitly framing together is taking place. In some kind of magical way, which no one ever sees we are all being knit together, fitly framed together. The Bible says that we are to grow together, we are to be fitly framed together, and we are to be built together as a home of God in the Spirit. In other words, we have to give diligence to keep this unity of the Spirit.

It is not enough that we should see the oneness of Christ. The next thing we have to do is commit ourselves to the oneness of Christ and then be prepared for all the many difficulties, limitations, and problems that will come in the process of being perfected into one. Oh, if only it was one of those wonderful instant things that you have over here—instant cream, instant coffee, instant lemon tea, and I don't know what else. It would be lovely if we could have this kind of instant perfection into oneness. But it is here that we have all our problems. It is much easier to be one with the saints in Melbourne, Australia than one with the saints in our own locality.

I am always hearing people say, "Oh, it is so wonderful to be in the body of Christ," and what they mean by the body of Christ is the saints in Africa, Asia, Australia, South America, and the other side of the United States. But the whole thing comes down to where you live. It is no good saying, "I believe in the oneness of Christ," if we do not recognise that oneness where we live. Somehow or other we are to be built together in that area in which we live because the whole thing finally comes down to where we live. Whatever we might feel about locality, the fact of the matter is that in the end all spiritual things come down to your body, and your body is located on this earth. It comes down to your home and your home is located in some place on the earth. It comes down to the company of believers where you live in some locality on this earth. It stands to reason.

I can talk till I am blue in the face about going on with the Lord and the whole thing can be some kind of pipe dream. It is all up there in the clouds. We have all met people who talk and talk and talk and talk and who have nothing in their lives of the practice. They live in some kind of fool's paradise, some kind of day dreaming all the time. God brings it all down to the matter of where we live and the believers that are in the same area in which we live, and how we are getting on with them, and in what way we are being built together.

Well, you say, "That is not so easy because in the area in which I live there are Episcopalians, Baptists, and Methodists, and this, that, and the other, and they will not come together." But there may be some, who at least see something of the oneness of Christ, and with whom you can move together and fellowship together and be built together. We do not shut out other people; we include them. The church is not exclusive; it is inclusive, and this has been one of the great mistakes of church history. Every time people have seen something they have become exclusive instead of inclusive, instead of taking in the whole family of God, and saying, "If they want to go their way we cannot stop them, but we will put no barriers up. They belong to us and we belong to them.

We will love them, and we will serve them, and if necessary we will lay down our lives for them."

Some people have this attitude: "If a person is a believer but a Baptist, I am not going to lay down my life for him; that would be a waste. If someone is a believer who has really seen something, I will lay down my life for him." But that is not the cross. The cross is that the Lord Jesus laid down His life for us all. The vast majority of those of us who have been saved are a load of trouble to Him. We do not progress as we ought to progress. We do not grow as we ought to grow. But He laid down His life for us all. May the Lord help us to see this basis of our fellowship in practical terms and see that there has to be some perfecting into that oneness. There has got to be some building. There has got to be some growing up into the Head from whom the whole body fitly framed and knit together through that which every joint supplies, according to the working in due measure of each part, maketh the increase of the body unto the building up of itself in love (see Ephesians 4:15–16).

The Great Variety in Unity

That leads me to another point I would like to make, and that is the great variety there is in this unity. Now suffer me for a few moments on this matter. It is an extraordinary thing in the history of God's work and of the church, how as soon as real men of God begin to see something of the nature of God's purpose, in the end they reduce the whole thing to a uniformity. They seem to equate unity with uniformity. Now many of these would be the first to deny it and say, "No, no, no, we believe that there is diversity in unity." But when it comes to it, we all have to do what they say. We all have to think what they think. We all have to act as they act. We all have to almost clothe ourselves with their clothes. We are not permitted to be original people. We all have to be little uniform copies of some master pattern. You see it again and again and again.

Take the Quakers. Was there ever a movement of the Spirit of God like the Quakers? But before very long it was all "thee"s and "thou"s and buckles on hats and buckles on shoes. Now if there are any Quakers here, forgive me, but you know what I mean.

Then there were the Mennonites—no buttons and certain clothes. Thank God for the Mennonites! What a movement of God it was! But it was reduced to uniformity. I can tell Pentecostals by the way they pray. Most of them are like planes taking off on a runway. They sort of rev up like the old propeller type, and they umm, uummm, uumMM, uuUUMMMM! At home, I can even tell you the kind of Pentecostal by the way they pray. It is amazing the uniformity we get.

Somehow or other we have to reduce everything to a system, everything to a structure, everything to a kind of uniformity. But in this unity of Christ there is tremendous variety, and tremendous diversity, and tremendous originality. Never be afraid of being yourself. God can never be Himself until you are yourself, and God can never be Himself in a company of people till every member of the body of Christ is himself or herself. When we all ape one another and try to be one another we do terrible damage to the whole work of the Spirit of God in really building up the body of Christ. Whole movements of the Spirit of God, such as the Exclusive Brethren, have gone right off the rail on this issue. They have reduced everything to such a uniformity that they have lost the headship of Jesus Christ, and found the headship of men.

We must be built together, and in being built together we have to sacrifice our individuality or perhaps it would be more correct to say our individualism. We must know a certain limitation. How can one stone be built together next to another stone and have another stone on top and another stone already underneath without feeling some claustrophobic sense? There is a limitation in fellowship. There is a discipline in fellowship. There is something that gets at the very root of the Fall, in this whole matter of fellowship, which is that we want to be our untouched selves. But having said that, our being built together and all the discipline and limitation of fellowship must never be at the expense of variety and originality.

Isn't it interesting that at the beginning of all these movements of the Spirit of God there has been such an expression sometimes, for instance, in poetry, in hymnology, in songs, in all kinds of things because everyone under the government of the church can, together, express the Lord in an original way. But as time goes on you find less and less and less and less. And when you do get anything written, it is hideous because it is just the party line.

Eccentricity

Now I must say a word of warning. What about eccentricity? God in His great mercy has saved a number of eccentrics. Every company of the Lord's people has within it eccentrics, nor should we throw them out because they are eccentric.

Some eccentrics (and I could keep you here for an hour or two telling you stories about eccentrics I know) have been really used of the Lord in their strange eccentric way. Nevertheless, we must never think that originality is eccentricity. There is within all of us some desire to be exhibitionists even those who are introspective; it is only pride that so often makes them hang back in the background. Really, they are just as much an exhibitionist as the rest of us. They are only a little afraid of it because they are afraid they might make a mistake in their exhibitionism and sort of blow the gap.

We ought to be careful of eccentrics, and at the same time receive them, but this oneness of Christ does not mean we just put up with anything. There is a discipline in the body of Christ, and there are times when the brethren have to speak to someone whose eccentricity is damaging the testimony of the Lord. We have seen eccentrics in our own company who have really been modified and adjusted. They are still eccentrics because God saved the eccentric, but they are modified and kept in check without destroying their originality.

Every one of us is different, and every one of us has something to give. We have different backgrounds, different temperaments, and different emphases. If we had John Newton with us, could he do anything else but accentuate the grace of God? His very background and his temperament must mean his emphasis is the grace of God. Whenever we meet together in some way or another you will find that his contribution is somehow or other always related to the grace of God. There are other people who in the most wonderful way have something to give; maybe it is the love of God. They are always overwhelmed by the love of

God, and they have this to give because their very background, their very temperament, everything somehow has led them to an appreciation of the love of God. We all appreciate the love of God, but they have something to give in this matter. Do you understand? God forbid that we would all be the same.

In our company we have those who believe in predestination. They are normally called Calvinists and I am one of them. There are others who are Armenians, that is, they believe in free will. We have never fought. I am free to simply say that I believe firmly in the sovereignty of God in all things. Others go on talking about the responsibility of man and the free will. We need each other. I do not see how people can be anything else than a Calvinist when something happens to them.

I had a friend, long since now gone to be with the Lord. He was a captain in the Merchant Navy, and he got drunk. He did not want God, but in his drunken stupor God appeared to him. When he came out with a hangover he was saved. That man became a Calvinist. What else? Could he be anything else? It was stupid to say to him, "Ah, but you are in error." The man had been converted in a drunken stupor. What is even more amazing is that his dear wife, who over-lived him by quite a few years and has only recently gone to the Lord, was so puzzled by this amazing change in his behaviour, that she said to me, "I was sweeping up dust in the hall and I suddenly leant on top of the broom and suddenly I was converted. I was just standing thinking, 'What ever has happened to Charles?'" She got saved! Of course, they became outstanding Calvinists.

Someone else has gotten saved by going forward in a meeting, and it has been just as real a conversion. He naturally sees the need for man to respond and for man's responsibility. He sees it!

Don't you see that in this oneness of Christ there is place for both of us? We are all too small to contain the infinity of God. We cannot do it, however much people think. I always take that little hymn: "Come and Rejoice With Me" because the last verse says, "And now I know it all," which I think adequately sums up some Christians. They give the impression that "Now I know it all." But however much we know, we only know in part, and what I see has to be tempered by what you see, and what I give has to be, as it were, tempered by what you give.

I used to wonder when I was first saved why there was a Matthew, a Mark, a Luke, and a John. I was always wondering because when I was saved, I had never read my Bible, and I knew nothing about it. But when I got hold of a whole Bible and began to read it, I was very, very amazed by Matthew, Mark, Luke, and John, especially when I heard from some Christians that there were contradictions. It was quite extraordinary because they told me it is the Word of God, authoritative and inspired—and yet that there are contradictions. So I went to a godly old man in the church and asked him all about it. He said, "Yeah, well you see Matthew reveals Christ as King. Mark reveals Christ as Servant. Luke reveals Christ as Man, and John reveals Christ as God. Then I said to him: "I cannot understand that." Being a very irreverent youngster, (I was only 13), I said to him, "I do not understand that because if I had been God I would have taken John because you say he is the most spiritual. Why couldn't John have written the whole lot and revealed Christ as King, Christ as

Servant, Christ as Man, and Christ as God? Then you would not have this contradiction. Of course, he gave me up; he thought I was a hopeless case.

I still believed in the authority and inspiration of the Bible. It was only many years later that I came to see that when God wanted to reveal Christ as King, He took Matthew who was an income tax inspector and knew a lot about kings and government and institutions like that. From his very conservative Hebrew background, being from the tribe of Levi, he was able to express Christ as King. Mark, as we often say, was the voice of Peter and the hands of Mark. The fact of the matter is that it was through Peter the fisherman that we see Christ as the Servant of the Lord. Then He takes Doctor Luke and reveals Christ as Man, through a man who understood anatomy and something of the make-up of man. Finally he takes John and reveals Christ as God. Now when you bring Matthew, Mark, Luke, and John together you have fullness. When you divide them, you have fragmented the unity.

You know, our churches are all Matthews over here, Marks over there, Lukes over here, and Johns over there. We have fragmented the unity of Christ. When we bring them together, we have fullness. All of us are Matthews, or Marks, or Lukes, or Johns. We have it everywhere. You can still tell the difference between the apostle Paul and the apostle James in the very style of writing. You can tell the difference between the apostle John and the apostle Peter in their style of writing. So if it is inspiration, how come it is not uniform? How come all these styles have not been overcome by the Spirit of God? It is because the Spirit of God does not bypass human personality but expresses Himself through human personality. That is why. Pagan inspiration is always the bypassing of the mind; that is spiritistic. Mediums go out and say things and they do not even know what they are saying. But inspiration, true inspiration, the exercise of spiritual gifts, is always under the control of the prophets. "The spirits of the prophets are subject to the prophets" (1 Corinthians 14:32). They may not always understand exactly the meaning of what they say, but they do know the words they are using. They inquired as to what the Spirit of Christ in them did mean when He signified these things. They were not just blotto, fizzled out, unconscious, and being sort of manipulated by the Spirit of God, but that is the idea some people have. No, not at all! When the Spirit of God gets into us, He takes us all.

I believe there are things that Paul would never have written if he had realised that it was Scripture. Do you think the apostle Paul would have put down things like this: "Oh, you are making me boast all you" (see II Corinthians 10:8) or in another place where he said, "I was sorry about that first letter I wrote you. I wept buckets of tears over it, and then I got your second letter and I realised all was okay" (see II Corinthians 2). If he had known that thousands and thousands of Christians all down through the generations were going to read it, he may have said, "Oh, I must cut that out and cut that out." But you see when the Spirit of God came through the apostle Paul, we find that the apostle Paul comes over as well. We find a man is there. He is disciplined. He is broken. He is joined to the Lord, but it is still Paul. It is still Peter. It is still James. It is still John. That is what we need if we are to really know the oneness of

Christ—an interdependence upon one another in the right way, and yet originality, variety, and diversity in this oneness.

Recognise the Unity of the Spirit

I will mention four things in the maintenance of this unity which is so essential. The first is recognition. Romans 12:3–6 says, "For I say, through the grace that was given me, to every man that is among you, not to think of himself more highly than he ought to think; but so to think as to think soberly, according as God hath dealt to each man a measure of faith. For even as we have many members and these members have not the same office: so, we who are many, are one body in Christ, and severally members one of another. And having gifts differing according to the grace that was given to us, if prophecy, let us prophesy according to the proportion of our faith."

We shall never be able to maintain the unity of the Spirit until we first recognise the unity of the Spirit. In other words, this may sometimes cost us everything to recognise the unity of the Spirit. I cannot touch things that are division. I love all the people of God, but I cannot become a Baptist. I cannot be a Methodist. I cannot be an Episcopalian. I cannot touch those things that divide the body of Christ, but I belong to the people of God within them. I will serve them to my last day. I belong to them and they belong to me. We are the Israel of God. We are one, not we ought to be one; we are one. I start on that basis. I do not look at my sister and say, "Shall I have her as my sister or not?" I start on the basis that she is my sister. We have problems at times, especially in the past, but she is my sister. She is my flesh and blood. I belong to her and she belongs to me. We are in the same family. So we must recognise every true child of God as a member of the family. They may not exactly be to our liking, but they are our brothers and our sisters and we have to love them and serve them.

Receive One Another

The second thing is we must receive one another. That is Romans 15:7 and compare that with Romans 14:1: "Him that is weak in the faith receive ye yet not for investigation of his conscience." Oh my, don't we go into that sometimes! As soon as we find a new believer we want to find out if they have been baptized. Have they had an experience of the Holy Spirit? Do they know what holiness is? Are they separated from the world? We investigate their conscience, and if we feel they do not have too much of a conscience we will give them one. We will make up for any deficiency of conscience by making sure that they are quite clear as to what is right and what is wrong in these things; we cannot leave them to the Spirit of God. But we are to receive one another as also Christ received us.

There is another verse in Philippians 3:16b: "Only, whereunto we have attained, by that same rule let us walk." In other words, don't you come down from what God has done with you. If God has brought you to a certain point, you stay there because God has dealt with you, but do not expect everybody else to immediately be brought to that same level. God may have dealt with you for a particular reason. You obey the Lord and go on with Him and love the rest.

Give Diligence to Keep the Unity

The third thing is godly maintenance, and this means we have to work on this matter. Ephesians 4:3 says, "Giving diligence, to keep the unity of the Spirit in the bond of peace." In other words, you cannot just leave it as a vague, abstract matter. You have got to give diligence to keep it. Now that may cost you an awful lot at times. There are times when you feel someone has got something against you and you may have to go to him or her and say, "What is it?" There are other times when you have got something against someone else, and after you have sought the Lord, you have got to go and get that settled. But keep the unity of the Spirit.

Remember what our Lord said, "If ye forgive one another your heavenly Father will also forgive you, but if ye forgive them not their trespasses, neither will your heavenly Father forgive you," Matthew 6:14, 15. Remember He taught us to pray in the pattern prayer: "Forgive us our trespasses as we forgive those who trespass against us," Matthew 6:12. That is a tremendous thing to pray; for we are praying that God will only forgive us in the measure in which we forgive others. Our Lord took this one thing out of the whole pattern prayer and said, "This is the most important thing of all, and He put it first in the positive, then in the negative. He said, "If you forgive men their trespasses I will forgive you. If you forgive not, neither will your Father forgive you." Isn't that tremendous! That brings you immediately to the tremendous importance of this matter of the oneness of Christ.

Openness in Fellowship

Lastly, the fourth one is openness. 1 John 1:7 says, "If we walk in the light as God is in the light, we have fellowship one with another, and the blood of Jesus Christ God's Son cleanses us from all sin." You cannot maintain fellowship when you are doing things in the dark. Sometimes people have all kinds of things and they will not bring them out in the open, they will not bring them out for fellowship, they will not bring them out in the light; they hide them. They are so afraid of what their brothers and sisters will do if they bring it out into the open. Sometimes it is not something dark or wrong. Sometimes it is just a question of career, or job, or where a person is going to go. They are so afraid to bring it out in the open and share it because they feel that somehow or other maybe we will dictate to them or do this or this or this. Never! We must walk in the light as God is in the light, and then we have fellowship one with another.

Shall we pray?

Dear Lord, Thou knowest just how fundamental and essential this principle of unity is in the matter of fellowship. Lord, wilt Thou take all that has been said and get it into our hearts. Where there is already some understanding, oh, give greater understanding, and where there has been no understanding of this matter, Lord let Thy light shine in and give, we pray, an understanding of this whole matter. We want to be a people who give diligence to keep the unity of the Spirit in the bond of peace. We want to know that increasing with the increase of God. We want to know the body building up itself in love. Oh Lord, help us and if there are things that are wrong amongst us, give us grace and help us to put those things right. We ask it together in the name of our Lord Jesus Christ. Amen.

3.
Principles of Fellowship–Continuity

Zechariah 4:1–10

And the angel that talked with me came again, and waked me, as a man that is wakened out of his sleep. And he said unto me, What seest thou? And I said, I have seen, and, behold, a lampstand all of gold, with its bowl upon the top of it, and its seven lamps thereon; there are seven pipes to each of the lamps, which are upon the top thereof; and two olive-trees by it, one upon the right side of the bowl, and the other upon the left side thereof. And I answered and spake to the angel that talked with me, saying, What are these, my lord? Then the angel that talked with me answered and said unto me, Knowest thou not what these are? And I said, No, my lord. Then he answered and spake unto me, saying, This is the word of the Lord unto Zerubbabel, saying, Not by might, nor by power, but by my Spirit, saith the Lord of hosts. Who art thou, O great mountain? Before Zerubbabel thou shalt become a plain; and he shall bring forth the top stone

*with shoutings of Grace, grace,
unto it. Moreover the word of
the Lord came unto me, saying,
The hands of Zerubbabel have
laid the foundation of this
house; his hands shall also finish
it; and thou shalt know that the
Lord of hosts hath sent me unto
you. For who hath despised the
day of small things? for these
seven shall rejoice, and shall
see the plummet in the hand of
Zerubbabel; these are the eyes of
the Lord, which run to and fro
through the whole earth.*

Matthew 16:18–19

*And I also say unto thee, that
thou art Peter, and upon this
rock I will build my church;
and the gates of Hades shall
not prevail against it. I will
give unto thee the keys of
the kingdom of heaven: and
whatsoever thou shalt bind on
earth shall be bound in heaven;
and whatsoever thou shalt*

*loose on earth shall be loosed in
heaven.*

Revelation 10:1–7

*And I saw another strong angel
coming down out of heaven,
arrayed with a cloud; and the
rainbow was upon his head, and
his face was as the sun, and
his feet as pillars of fire; and
he had in his hand a little book
open: and he set his right foot
upon the sea, and his left upon
the earth; and he cried with a
great voice, as a lion roareth:
and when he cried, the seven
thunders uttered their voices.
And when the seven thunders
uttered their voices, I was
about to write: and I heard a
voice from heaven saying, Seal
up the things which the seven
thunders uttered, and write
them not. And the angel that I
saw standing upon the sea and
upon the earth lifted up his right
hand to heaven, and sware by*

him that liveth for ever and ever, who created the heaven and the things that are therein, and the earth and the things that are therein, and the sea and the things that are therein, that there shall be delay no longer: but in the days of the voice of the seventh angel, when he is about to sound, then is finished the mystery of God, according to the good tidings which he declared to his servants the prophets.

I feel I have a particular burden to do with fellowship but will need all the Lord's grace in order to discharge, and will need all the Lord's grace for you to really hear what He says. Shall all of us unite together in really taking hold of the Lord and standing into that anointing which is ours in the Lord Jesus Christ, made available to us by the Spirit of God for this time.

Shall we bow together?

Oh Father, we come to Thee as Thy children whom Thou hast redeemed through the precious blood of our Lord Jesus Christ and we thank Thee for all that Thou art to us. Lord, now as we come we pray that as we turn to Thy Word, Thou wilt make it living and active, Thou wilt make it to be something that is a ministry of life from Thy throne to all of us. Oh Lord, Thou knowest this burden that I have, and I believe it is from Thee. Help me to discharge it. Open a door of utterance to speak this mystery of Christ and give us ears to hear by Thy Spirit what Thou art saying. Quiet the children, Lord, and every other noise or anything else that would be used by the enemy to somehow make it difficult for Thee to get through to us. Lord, we hold this time before

Thee, and we thank Thee that there is an anointing for it. We thank
Thee that Thou hast made a provision of grace for it. Lord, we would
exploit that grace and take hold of it for speaker and hearer alike. We
commit ourselves to Thee. In the name of our Lord Jesus Christ. Amen.

There is one other little phrase in Deuteronomy 8:2 that I would like to mention: "And thou shalt remember all the way which the Lord thy God hath led thee these forty years in the wilderness, that he might humble thee, to prove thee, to know what was in thy heart, whether thou wouldest keep his commandments, or not." I would like to underline that little word: "... thou shalt remember all the way which the Lord thy God hath led thee."

We have been talking about fellowship, the principles of fellowship, and something of the true meaning of fellowship. We have discovered that fellowship is not just something surface or superficial, but is, in its deepest and most substantial sense, the sharing of our Lord Jesus Christ. "God is faithful, through whom ye were called into the fellowship of his Son Jesus Christ our Lord" (1 Corinthians 1:9). That does not mean, of course, that the Lord Jesus has lost His unique position. He is still God the Son, but we, joined to Him have become the new man, and in this marvelous sense we have been brought into a union with God in and through our Lord Jesus Christ and a union with one another. We have come into an eternal relationship with God and an eternal relationship with one another in Him.

We spoke on the principle of unity, and really what I want to say now is an expansion and an extension of that principle of unity—not a regulation but a principle. It is something which is cause and effect. If we obey that principle of unity, then there are certain consequences, certain results. We spoke of the oneness of all God's people here on earth, our oneness with believers where we live, and so on.

The Communion of Saints

What I want to speak about now is not so easy to put in a word or two, but it is what I call the principle of continuity, and it is very rarely recognised or understood by the people of God. It seems to me that it is the ignorance of this principle, which is the undoing of many, many real and genuine movements of the Spirit of God. God starts to do something very real amongst His people, but because those dear believers, we believers do not understand that we are essentially and organically bound up with all that has gone before, we make some terrible mistakes. There are some tragedies. The Lord says in one connection, "Remember not the former things; I will do a new thing," (see Isaiah 43:18,19a). Because all of us love to be in something that is new, we forget that there are times when God says to us, "Thou shalt remember all the way that the Lord Thy God has led thee," (see Deuteronomy 8:2a).

Of course, we do not recite the creed together, but there is a phrase in the earliest of all the creeds that Christians recite, and it is this: "I believe in the communion of saints." What does that mean? It means simply this: we are not only one with all who are in Christ on this earth now, but we are one in Christ with all whom God has brought into Him from time immemorial. Isn't that wonderful! That means we are organically one with all the saints who are gathered into the presence of the Lord. God has been doing only one thing. The history of the church is not a whole series of little things that God has been doing, sort of doing a little thing here and doing a little thing there. This century He does something and it breaks down. Then He does this in another century and it breaks down. Then He starts again here and it breaks down, and it has no relationship with the rest. What God has been doing is an essential entity. It is something which began at the cross, its dynamic at Pentecost, and God has never stopped working that work to this very day. Every single saint, whatever their colour, whatever their race, whatever their nationality, whatever part of the globe they happen to live in, if they have been saved by the grace of God, in any time, historically, as well as tonight, all those who have been brought into Christ are one body. There is only one church. It is a vital principle.

The Problem of Superiority

As I have already said, it is because of ignorance of this principle that many, many moves of the Spirit of God have been undone and finally nullified and destroyed. We have not understood this principle of continuity. I do hope that by the grace of God I am able to put over quite clearly what I mean.

So often I find that where the Lord has really started to show something to His people, especially younger people, and we are bowled over by what we see, we tend to get this idea that everything else has failed but us. You know that kind of attitude: "Everything else has failed. The Methodists failed. The Quakers failed. The Puritans failed. The Moravians failed. The Brethren failed. The Pentecostals have failed miserably. Everyone has failed but us. We have seen! We have seen! We are a new thing; we are the new thing of God!" We put a little circle around ourselves and we get very superior about it: "Everything else in the history of the church has failed but us." This is an invitation for God to leave us to the enemy's work; for once we do this we uncover ourselves in the most terrible way. It is just like on a personal level when the Lord Jesus said to Peter: "Simon, Simon, Satan has obtained thee by request, but I have prayed for thee that thy faith fail not," (see Luke 22:31,32a). He uncovered himself by making a claim from his own flesh life. "I will die with You, Lord, if I have to" he said, "but I will never deny You" (see Matt 26:35a) and in that moment he uncovered himself.

In the same way corporately we often get into this trap where we think we are sort of succeeding where everything else has failed in the history of the church. We are, as it were, the unique work of God. I sometimes get letters sent to me by people who tell me that nothing has happened in a certain part of the world for a century or more, and that now something tremendous has happened. Then I wait for them to collapse because I have never known anyone to make such a claim without them being after a year or two completely bowled over and destroyed.

Our problem is that sometimes we think that we have no link with anything that has gone before, nothing at all. We have nothing really to learn from what has gone before, and we have no organic link. If we do we only learn from it as a kind of historical object lesson. We do not understand that they are part of us and we are part of them, and all that God has done down through the ages is an essential unity. Where were the early Methodists? In Christ. Where were the early Quakers? In Christ. Where were the Puritans? In Christ. Where were the Reformers? In Christ. Where were the Brethren? In Christ. And so are we. It is something that binds us together. Ignorance of this principle often leads to rejection of all the values of the past, as if what God is doing in our generation has got to be unique in the sense that it draws nothing at all from the values and heritage of the past.

I feel sorry sometimes when we do not sing some of the old hymns that represent the values of what God has done in the history of the church. I know some of them are antiques and some are best read, but there are some which I must say represent the choicest and most wonderful values that God wrought in His people in that day and age. It belongs to us. It is not just that we are singing something antique; we are expressing something that we have come into by the grace of God. It has cost the Lord and His people everything to recover those truths which are now household words with us.

The Problem of Innovations

Another one of the problems is innovation. Have you noticed how so often one of the things the enemy tries to do in new moves of God is to bring innovation in, things that have never at any time been amongst the people of God from the day of Pentecost till today? Sometimes they are weird things. Sometimes they are things that are somehow hooked on some obscure passage of the Word of God and twisted and explained, and then you have an innovation which sweeps through everything. We find it again and again and again, as if somehow or other we have to find something which is novel, something which has never been done before, something which is unique, something which tempts us as a unique work of God. But my dear friend, that is not what God is doing. There is a sense in which every single thing we come into has already been in the church. There is nothing new under the sun in this matter.

People sometimes think that speaking in a tongue is somehow a new thing. My dear friend, they are ignorant of church history. People tell me it died with the early church. When did it die with the early church? The Montanists spoke in tongues. The Waldensians spoke in tongues. The Bogomils spoke in tongues. The Paulicians spoke in tongues. The Anabaptists spoke in tongues and some of the Huguenots. The prophets of the Cevennes spoke in tongues. The early Methodists spoke in tongues. The Quakers spoke in tongues. Where is all this nonsense?

Is baptism something that came in with the late 19th century? Never! The Waldensians practiced baptism. The Bogomils practiced baptism. The Paulicians practiced baptism. (Now you are getting befogged by all of these marvellous names.) There is nothing new about it. The Anabaptists, in the 15th and 16th century were drowned by the thousands in the fountains of Central Europe, sewed up in sacks, mothers and children flung into the rivers. But baptism by immersion for believers is a household word amongst the people of God now. Even some Episcopalians slink away to some Baptist place to get baptized and Presbyterians and Methodists. We recognise it. But when the enemy is seeking to undo something because of our ignorance of this principle of continuity, he presses in with innovations, things that have never been known before from the beginning until now. By those things he seeks to divide and destroy the people of God in that generation.

The Continuous and Consistent Work of God

Now I do not want to be on the negative side; I want to be on the positive side. What I am saying is this: We have a tremendous heritage! Brothers and sisters, dear family of God, it is the most wonderful privilege to be alive in the last half of the 20th century. There are people who tell me they would have given their right arm to have been there on the day of Pentecost. I wouldn't. Who wants to be there on the day of Pentecost? I think it is simply tremendous that we are here in the last part of the 20th century, don't you? They were starting out, and it was wonderful when they were starting out and to see all the wonderful works of God and the power of God, the signs and the miracles authenticating the ministry and the gospel. But I find it even more wonderful that we should come at the end of the age and have behind us a heritage, which has cost the blood and life of thousands of God's choicest overcomers. Shall we trample it underfoot? Shall we treat it as refuse? Shall we look upon it as nothing to do with us, just a little historical illustration of the power of God in such and such a century? Or did God do something then which is essentially part of what He is doing today? Only today He wants to lead us on just that step further. With all that other fullness behind us, with all that heritage behind us, He wants to take us on to the last step that will result in the coming of our Lord and the top stone going into place.

One of the prophets once said to the children of Israel as it is recorded in Isaiah 51:1–3: "Hearken to me, ye that follow after righteousness, ye that seek the Lord: look unto the rock whence ye were hewn, and to the hole of the pit whence ye were digged. Look unto Abraham your father, and unto Sarah that bare you; for when he was but one I called him, and I blessed him, and made him many. For the Lord hath comforted Zion; he hath comforted all her waste places, and hath made her wilderness like Eden, and her desert like the garden of the Lord; joy and gladness shall be found therein, thanksgiving, and the voice of melody."

I am asking you to remember all the way that the Lord our God has led us from the day of Pentecost. Of course, if I had the time I would like to go right back to father Abraham and start there, and well we might and go right the way through the whole Old Testament and into the New, but we do not have time to do that. The fact of the matter is that God has been doing something all the way through the centuries of this age, and the work that He has been doing is a continuous work; it is a consistent and continuous work. Within it therefore we shall find all the values that we need for the day and age in which we live. Why should we be like an illustration of what Mark Twain said, "What we learn from history is that we never learn from history"? If the people of God would only understand the ways of the Lord, understand some of those ways by which He led His own through the centuries of this age, we would be saved from many, many tragedies and would become much more the wiser in our understanding of what God is doing in our own day.

The Testimony of Jesus

I would like to say something about the testimony of Jesus. You will notice in that prophecy of Zechariah 4 the first thing that Zechariah saw was a lampstand all of gold, and he was very taken with the olive tree on either side which fed the lampstand all of gold. Of course, I cannot go through all that substantiates the claim that the lampstand all of gold is a symbol of the testimony of Jesus, but I think most of us will recognise it. Later on in the book of Revelation, we find that it stands for seven churches, the church expressed in seven localities. However, we discover that it is not just the church because the lampstand could be removed, but the church's activities, its meetings, its routines could just rumble on and the lampstand be taken away. The lampstand is not just the outward paraphernalia of the church; the lampstand stands for our Lord Jesus Christ, the testimony that Christ is everything, and in Him is everything we need individually and corporately.

In Zechariah 4 we find that this lampstand stands for building. We immediately discover that the whole thing is to do with building. It is an extraordinary vision. The first thing that Zechariah sees is a great gold lampstand with its seven branches and its seven lamps for light and then an olive tree on the left hand and on the right hand. Then he sees their pipes feeding gold from the olive tree into the lampstand. It is extraordinary. He says to the angel, "What are these, Lord?" Meaning the olive tree because he had some feeling that the olive tree was to do with him; we are all so self-centered. "What are these, Lord?" he said to the angel. He forgot the lampstand altogether; he was more interested in where he came into the picture. "What are these?" The angel said, "This is the word of the Lord to Zerubbabel, saying, Not by might, nor by power, but by my Spirit, saith the Lord of hosts. Who art thou, O great mountain? Before Zerubbabel thou shalt become a plain; and he shall bring forth the top stone with shoutings of Grace, grace, unto it. Moreover the word of the Lord came unto me, saying, The hands of Zerubbabel have laid the foundation of this house; his hands shall also finish it" (Zechariah 4:6–9a).

We suddenly discover to our amazement that this lampstand is not something static, but it represents a building work of God, a building programme of God, something that God is doing in His people, in His redeemed ones. He is calling them out of every nation and kindred and tongue and people and doing something in them whereby Christ becomes in them everything. If we had the time we could talk much more about it, but it comes down to locality. It comes down to the area in which we live and our relatedness with one another. But what I am trying to say simply is that this lampstand is not some abstract glorious ideal that is set before the church. It is not some beautiful, ethereal thing somewhere up there in the heavenlies that no one ever sees but invisibly is taking place. It is a building programme that God is engaged in with living stones being built together upon a foundation, and so as the building goes up the Word of the Lord comes to Zerubbabel: "Who art thou, O great mountain? Before Zerubbabel thou shalt become a plain; and the top stone, the last stone of the whole building programme, the top stone shall come forth with shoutings of Grace, grace, unto it."

I have always been amazed at the word, grace, grace and not glory, glory. Good Charismatics, I suppose would all feel that the shouts should be, "Glory! Glory! God has done it! A great crest like a tidal wave has come in and the work has been finished!" But I think there will be such a conflict, such intense pressure, so many complex problems that when the building is ready for the top stone, who is the Messiah, all we shall be able to say when we see the Messiah is, "The grace of God has completed the work. Grace began it, grace developed it, grace kept it moving, and grace has completed the work."

The Organic Union of the Body of Christ

We read of the mystery of God in Ephesians 3:4–6. Again, it is all to do with the testimony of Jesus. We find it for instance in these words: "Whereby, when ye read, ye can perceive my understanding in the mystery of Christ; which in other generations was not made known unto the sons of men, as it hath now been revealed unto his holy apostles and prophets in the Spirit; to wit, that the Gentiles are fellow-heirs, and fellow-members of the body, and fellow-partakers of the promise in Christ Jesus through the gospel."

What a wonderful thing this mystery is! It has been hid. I believe that God started this whole work with Abraham and that the saints of the Old Covenant are indissolubly joined to us. Not only that, God has held them back that they should not be made perfect without us, and we have been brought in. Isn't that wonderful! Nevertheless, it is a new thing that God is doing in one sense. What is the new thing? Whereas in the Old Covenant the body was not revealed, its organic entity was not revealed, now it has been revealed by the Spirit of God. The coming of the Holy Spirit has brought the whole thing from outside to within, and we are joined to the Lord and joined to one another in an organic union in Christ.

The Purpose of God Shall Prevail

What a wonderful thing it is that the book of Revelation tells us that the mystery of God is completed. It says in the sounding of the seventh angel that the mystery of God is completed. Thank God, the battle over the mystery is going to be completed! The Lord is going to win this great battle. The purpose of God has never at any time been annulled or even frustrated. Jesus said, "Upon this rock I will build My church, and the gates of hell shall not prevail against it," (Matthew 16:18b). In some of the versions it says, "the gates of Hades." The Revised Standard Version and other modern translators put "the power of death" because "gates of Hades" is a difficult idea. What it means is this: gates are the strongest point, in one sense, in the wall. The walls are strong, but the gates are also very massive and strong. It was within the gates that the elders used to sit for judgment, and it came to represent judgment or counsel. So here we have the very judgment or counsels of hell. I think the King James Version is quite right to use the word Hell rather than Hades because really the idea is of death. What is the weapon of Satan? What is his supreme weapon when he fights the building work of Christ? It is death—death, death, and more death. That is how he always works, and we have here the very counsels of death. If you like, the Lord Jesus said, "Upon this rock I will build My church, and the counsel of Satan shall not prevail against it." The judgment of Hell shall not prevail against it. The will and design of Hell shall not prevail against it.

There is another way of looking at it, which is deliberately ambiguous. It could mean that when the church presses into enemy territory, the gates of Hell, the counsels of Hell to keep captives in its hold, shall not prevail. Isn't that wonderful! When hell comes against us, it is not going to prevail over us. When we, by the grace of God and by the command and the commission of our risen Lord, go into the very realm of Satan to take out captives, he will not be able to stop us.

Gates can be unlocked; gates can be locked up. "Unto thee have I given the keys of the kingdom of heaven," (see Matthew 16:19a). We must unlock gates at times and we must lock them up at other times. Oh, there is a battle over this purpose of our Lord. All the combined power and authority of Hell cannot deter our Lord Jesus from fulfilling His purpose to build the church. Christ's hands laid the foundation; His hands are going to finish the work. "Thanks be unto God who giveth us the victory through our Lord Jesus Christ," (see 1 Corinthians 15:57).

There are mountains before us; there have always been mountains before us. There were mountains of difficulty and complexity before the early church. The Jewish Hebrew side found it very difficult to sit down and have a meal even with the Gentile side that was saved. Even the apostle Peter got carried away at one point. Don't you call that a mountain of complexity? I do. Circumcision was another great problem; it was a mountain of complexity. Oh, they had so many problems. Sometimes they had immorality amongst them because the Gentiles coming in did not have the Law sort of burned into their beings as the Jewish side had. There were many, many problems. There have always been problems. Wouldn't you think those poor souls called the Waldensians had problems? It was those that caused the Roman Catholic Church to withhold the Word of God from the ordinary people because they said, "These wild, wild, wild fanatics have gotten wild by reading the Word of God." So they passed a decree that the ordinary people should not read the Word of God. Don't you call that a mountain of difficulty? I do. It does not matter what mountains have been before our Lord Jesus Christ in the fulfilment of His purpose to build the church, they have all become a plain. Not a single mountain has stood in the way of our Lord once He has moved forward in this fulfilling of His purpose.

When we look at the book of Revelation, we see false prophets, and beasts, and dragons, and visions of the most terrifying creatures, and worldwide systems that are anti-god and antichrist with supreme power seemingly. However, none of it stops the Lord Jesus from fulfilling His purpose and finally finishing the mystery, completing the mystery. It all comes to pass. In Revelation 22:13, Christ calls Himself: "the alpha and the omega, the beginning and the end, the first and the last."

Oh, dear child of God, see this principle of fellowship, the principle of continuity. Jesus said, "I am the Alpha and the Omega." Dear child of God we are all in between. He is the first and He is the last, and we are all in between. He is the beginning and He is the end, and dear child of God, we are all in between. Oh, to me it is such a thrill to think of those early ones who overcame by the blood of the Lamb and by the word of their testimony because they loved not their lives unto death (see Revelation 12:11). Whether they were Paulicians, or Bogomils, or Donatists, or Montanists, or Priscillianists, or Waldensians, or Reformers, or the Huguenots, or the Moravians, or Quakers, or Methodists, or Anabaptists, or Pentecostals, whoever they are, we are bound together with them. Jesus is the first and Jesus is the last. Jesus is the beginning and Jesus is the end. There is a continuity in this whole thing. We have behind us tremendous wealth—that which God has wrought in the members of His Son's body. It has cost them everything!

Jesus is the Amen

I very much love this title of our Lord Jesus in Revelation 3:14: "And to the angel of the church in Laodicea write: These things saith the Amen, the faithful and true witness, the beginning of the creation of God." I think it is unparalleled grace that when the Lord speaks to the church of Laodicea He reveals Himself as the Amen. Amen is the last word. You do not say anything beyond amen or shouldn't. Amen, and that is the end. I knew a little boy who used to think when he heard people say, "Amen" that it meant the end of everything. (He got the right idea.) So as soon as his parents began to talk too long with other friends he began to say, "Amen, amen, amen." He used to think that was the best way to shut them up because amen was the ultimate. Normally you understand that word as "even so, let it be." But amen comes from the Hebrew word that simply means "to have faith." When you say, amen, you are saying, "I have faith; faith, even so." Think about that the next time you say, amen.

Our Lord Jesus is the Amen to the purpose of God. Even if you haven't got faith, He has. Our Lord Jesus Christ is the One who is going to carry the purpose of God through to its fulfilment by the grace of God.

We are in something that God began at Pentecost by His Spirit through Christ's finished work. The prophecy of Joel was never completely fulfilled on the day of Pentecost. I think most of you know that. If you look at the prophecy of Joel in chapter 2 and compare it with Acts chapter 2, you have to come to the conclusion that it has not been fulfilled, for it speaks of "that great and notable day of the Lord." What does it mean then? It means that the Holy Spirit is to characterize the whole of this age. It is by the Holy Spirit that this age was ushered in on the day of Pentecost, and every single move right through the history of the church of God in this age has been initiated by the Holy Spirit. Whether it has been keeping alive something in the Dark Ages, or the recovery of something in the Reformation, or in the successive recoveries that have come since then, it has been the Holy Spirit who has taken hold of men and women and used them in recovery.

The Movements of God in History

I do not want to bore you all because I know that most people are frightened to death of history and especially Americans. Mind you, you are now coming of age. I do not wish to be superior, but of course you are coming of age, and increasingly you will be more and more interested in history if the Lord tarries.

I wish we could learn the lessons of history. I wish we could understand what God has done in history. Never at any moment, even in what is called the Dark Ages, has the testimony of Jesus been completely lost. It is a mistake to say that from the 2nd century after Christ until the Reformation everything was lost. It is just not true! An intensive and exhaustive study of the history of the church of God will reveal some of the most remarkable movements of the Spirit in the so-called Dark Ages.

The people called Montanists were the Charismatics of the 4th century. They shocked the Roman Catholic Church. Tertullian, the great church father, severed his connection with the institutional church as did many others and they joined the Montanists saying, "Where two or three are gathered together in our Lord Jesus Christ, there is the church." By the way, the Montanists never took the name Montanist; that was given to them by everybody else. The Donatists who came later did not take that name; it was given to them by others. Paulicians were very proud because they said they went right back to Paul himself, and so they called them Paulicians because they had such an understanding of the eternal purpose of God and the mystery of Christ as found in the Pauline letters. There were the Bogomils. That is just Bulgarian for "friend of God." It sounds dreadful, doesn't it? But they called them "the friends of God." All these were great movements.

The Priscillianists in the south of France, and in Spain, and Italy were one of the greatest moves of the church of God. These people saw certain principles. They saw that a congregation could not be bossed by any other congregation. They saw that there should be elders in charge of the congregation. They saw the Lord's Table as something that illustrated their fellowship together in Christ. In some of these connections they saw the matter of baptism, and this is all during the Dark Ages. We are normally told that not a thing happened there, and so much of the information we have about these people we can only glean from those who hated them and martyred them. You know as well as I do, when you read some of the little booklets that have been written about some of my friends and those whom I have gained so much from the Lord through, if that was all we had we would believe they were heretics. Thank God! I think of brother Sparks. We have his ministry as well as the little pamphlets that were written against him. All these names were given to them by other people and much of what has so far been understood about these people has come from sources that were violently against them and were out to blacken their name and to give the justification for their mass martyrdom. But dear, dear child of God, the fact of the matter is that in the darkest part of the Dark Ages the testimony of Jesus never at any single point died out. It was kept alive in different parts of Europe and Asia by the Spirit of God. There were movements of the Spirit that cost the lives of those who were in them to obey the Lord and to serve Him.

I would like to talk a good deal more about this, but time does not permit it. I would like to talk about the Waldenses and the Albigenses. I suppose most of you have heard of the Waldensian Church. You have an airline here called *Piedmont*, and it was to those valleys of the Piedmont that the Waldensians finally were driven and where they found their refuge. I understand that no atheist ever travels on *Piedmont*. I'm told that if you should get on as an atheist, you will never get off as an atheist, so they tell me. I asked a while ago about the Piedmont folk and I found out that they were Waldensians who came to settle here in the United States. Anyway, that is by the way.

The Reformation Era

The fact of the matter is that we find different moves of the Spirit of God all the way through the Dark Ages. When we come to the Reformation era, of course, we begin to see something much more wonderful. We will begin with John Wycliffe, and I can only give you a few thoughts about him here. In 1320 in Britain he was an Oxford don, and he was converted by reading the words of God in Latin. God did such a work in his heart that as he began to investigate all the various activities and traditions of the church, he became increasingly bothered that they did not size up to the Word of God. Fearlessly, he began to preach against various abuses of the church. He was hated for it. So much was John Wycliffe hated that they held a special council in London at which both the Archbishop of York and the Archbishop of Canterbury came, as well as all the bishops of England. They had well nigh decided to burn John Wycliffe as a heretic, but they adjourned for lunch. During that adjournment, London was hit by one of the only earthquakes that has ever hit London, and the bishops were so frightened that they never reconvened, and Wycliffe died in his bed much later.

Nevertheless, Wycliffe was the man who set Britain on fire, and they were called the Lollards. We do not know why they were called the Lollards, whether it was because they talked so much or whether it was because of the way they seemed to be drunk with the Spirit, we don't know. But this we know that they said, "If there are three men together in any place in Britain, two of them are bound to be Lollards." That was the common saying that went over the whole of Britain. The only thing the church could do with Wycliffe was to dig up his bones one hundred years after his death, desecrate them and throw them in the river. However, I do not think that worried John Wycliffe.

Jerome of Prague heard John Wycliffe and caught fire. He went back to Prague and began to preach in the University of Prague, one of the oldest universities of Europe. A young man, Jan Hus listened to him and caught fire, and that man was to go over the whole of Bohemia, modern Czechoslovakia and part of Germany. Everywhere he went people found God and began to gather together in simple gatherings in farmhouses and homes simply having fellowship together and listening to the Word of God, for John Wycliffe translated the Bible from Latin into English. That was the greatest gift he gave, and from that it began to go out everywhere. The church caught Jan Hus at Constance and burned him at the stake, but when they burned Jan Hus, they set Europe on fire. From then on the Reformation was under way.

William Tyndale in Britain made it his lifelong ambition to take the Bible from the original Greek and later from the Hebrew and put it into the language of the man in the street. A theologian was sent to convert him from his wicked ways, but he said to that theologian: "Ere long, I shall see that every ploughboy in England has the Bible in his mother tongue."

William Tyndale was hounded from Britain to Brussels, to Antwerp where finally he was caught, strangled, and burned. But before he died he prayed, "Oh God, open the king of England's eyes." He died in 1536, and in 1538 by royal proclamation a copy of the Bible in English was chained to a lectern in every parish church of England and Wales. The Bible that the whole establishment was so against, God got it into the hands of the people. Do you know that at one time there were appeals made to the king that he should do something about it because in church services people were so bored with the vicar that they left him preaching in the pulpit and went around the lectern and had one of their number read the Scriptures in English to them. They got more from the Word of God than the vicar.

Of course, Erasmus was another man whom we must mention here in this revelation, for God took hold of this man and as someone said, "Erasmus laid the egg that Martin Luther hatched." The point was that Erasmus gave us for the first time the Bible in our tongue from the original Greek. Until then every version had been from Jerome's old Latin. Now for the first time a Greek New Testament was put into the hands of people all over Europe. It was revolutionary. It was that Greek New Testament that William Tyndale translated into English and it has become really the basis of the King James Version.

When Martin Luther came, that man so hated by some—bold, stubborn, courageous—the Reformation was fully come. Nothing stopped Martin Luther. You will remember that by 1517 three things that caused controversy in the whole of the civilised world were household words and accepted by all true believers. The first is justification by faith in the work of the Lord Jesus Christ alone. Secondly, is the access of every redeemed person to God through the Lord Jesus Christ without the need of a priest. Thirdly, there is the sole authority of the Word of God in all affairs to do with the people of God.

Dear child of God, those three things we accept as bread and butter. Who argues about justification? Who gets heated about justification? I wish they did. Everyone accepts it. Everyone accepts that we can go to the holiest place of all without a priest, by the blood of Jesus that we can come before God and speak with Him immediately. All of us accept the supreme authority and inspiration of the Word of God, but it cost those men their lives, and it has come to us by the Spirit of God and been given to us so that it has become our bread and butter. We do not even argue about these things. God recovered something in the Reformation that was never to be lost again. To this very day it has not been lost. Oh, there may be people who do not preach justification, people who do not believe in the Word of God, but every true believer knows what justification is, do they not? Every true believer understands that the Word of God is authoritative and inspired.

The Puritans

Since that Reformation there have been so many other things. It would take us all night and all of tomorrow to deal adequately with those many, many moves of the Spirit of God; I can only touch on a few. There were what we call the Puritans. You folks here in the United States must thank God for those Puritans because it was the persecution of the Puritans that really sent those founding fathers across the Atlantic to these shores. The very best of the people of God were expelled into a life of suffering and of endurance, and they did it for the sake of our Lord. They could have so easily not sacrificed everything for just a few adjustments on principle, but they would not. They would not! The Puritans may be sneered at by some quarters, but they laid the foundation for us as the people of God that has never been taken away. They gave us a godliness and an aptitude for the things of God, which has permeated Christian things from that day to this.

Calvin and Knox were really the fathers of the Puritans, and we can divide the Puritans into three groups basically—the Presbyterians, the Congregationalists or Independents, and the Baptists. But in the very short time of that movement of the Spirit of God, they had split into four great groups—the Establishment, called the Evangelical Church, and these other groups. For one moment, just think of the three groups—Presbyterian, Congregationalist, and Baptist. They gave us something which has never been taken away. Isn't it an interesting thing now that all over our countries we are coming to recognise eldership as the recognised norm as far as God is concerned for the government of the people of God? Who gave us this innovation? Who recovered this truth? The Presbyterians. They were called Presbyterians because they believed in presbyters, elders. They believed that the church should be ruled by a court of elders, a plurality of elders.

The Congregationalists believed in the independence of every congregation. It was a fantastic view in the day that they set it forth. They believed that every congregation was a congregation consisting of the believers in any given locality that had no right to be bossed or dominated by any other congregation of believers. Oh, if only God had kept that thought alive! There is something that was recovered to us and cost the blood of many, the life of many. In some of these movements they have been flung on one side, and churches all over the place have been taken under the control of one or two or a group of individuals. But the Congregationalists saw that every single company of God's people locally constituted was independent and in direct liaison with God. They saw the need, of course, of fellowship between the companies, but not domination by one company over others.

Then we have the Baptists, and of course they practiced baptism by immersion. I hardly need to say that. In Holland, in Britain, and then in America, increasingly more and more of these dear ones gave us something which is now a household word.

The Quakers

Within a century after this great move of God the whole thing had died. It had become institutionalised and crystallised, formal and dead, and then God did a remarkable thing. A young man went everywhere through the Puritans seeking to find God, but he couldnot find God anywhere. He heard only their choirs, their singing, and their dead preaching. His name was George Fox. He took his New Testament in English and went out into the hills of Derbyshire. For three years, like a young hippie, he sought for God wandering up and down Britain until one day he said, "My heart burned and God showed me that Christ was my Saviour." George Fox had been converted.

Many evangelicals are very suspicious of the Quakers. They say they are not really true evangelicals; they are not really born again. Oh, it is rubbish! The Quakers were one of the greatest moves of the Spirit of God in the history of the church, for they taught us a tremendous truth for which I praise God, at least as far as I am concerned and many other believers, for it has never yet been lost. It is that the inward is far more important with God than all the outward in the whole world. What is needed is communion with God, not just bread and wine. What is needed is to know what it is to die with Christ and to live in His resurrection, not just baptism. What is needed is to know what it is to submit to one another, not just the elders. What we need to do is to be built together, not just have a nice church building.

Oh, the Quakers went everywhere, and they turned the world upside down. The Puritans hated them. But the Quakers recovered something that has never been lost, that the nature of the church is essentially an inward and organic thing. But the Quakers used to meet together and wait in silence, not like they do today with all that long silence and sentimentality—twittering birds and lovely sunsets and all that kind of thing. That was not the early Quakers. They met together as solid, sturdy, rough men, and they would wait in quietness before God. Before very long, someone would tremble with the power of God and would stand up and speak the Word of the Lord. Then someone would open up the Bible as they prayed and give a word from God. Then someone would prophecy, and then someone would worship God. They did not sing because they had a reaction against dead singing, as they called it. It is amazing to me that the Quakers got the same results as the Pentecostals. The Pentecostals also sometimes trembled and would shake, and yet they sing beautifully. But the Quakers did not believe in singing or music. Isn't it interesting?

The Moravians

One hundred years after that we had another great movement of God, which I can only touch upon—the Moravians. It began in Central Europe and was to be one of the most remarkable contributions of the Spirit of God for recovery in the history of the church. Up to then the Puritans had not really considered perhaps too much of the evangelistic mission of the church, but the Moravians saw something that no one else saw, not even the Quakers. They saw that there were people dying in outer darkness, and it was the commission of the church to take the gospel to them. They said, "We will choose the hardest parts of the earth." They went to the Arctic. They went to all the most difficult parts of the earth, and they died in their hundreds. The Moravians had a prayer meeting twenty-four hours a day, which lasted one hundred years. Now don't think I am exaggerating. They had an around the clock, twenty-four hour prayer meeting, which lasted one hundred years. They are all connected by the way. Do you see how they are connected? George Fox would never have had a Bible in English but for William Tyndale, and William Tyndale but for Erasmus. Erasmus would not have been awakened but for Jon Hus, Wycliffe and others.

The Early Methodists

We can see it all go round and round. Then suddenly we find there was a man who came over to these parts, a good Britisher. He came over here to convert you all on this side and especially the red Indians. His name was John Wesley. But in his journal he said, "Oh God, I have come to convert the Indians, but who will convert me?" On the way over in the ship, he heard singing in the most terrible storm, and even the captain was terrified. Wesley said that he would not admit it, but he was frightened, and he went down to the bowels of the ship. As he went down he heard singing, and he thought, "Oh, it must be heaven." He looked through a door and he saw a whole group of Moravians, men, women, and children, just as if it were a drawing room meeting. They were sitting there singing hymns as if there was no danger at all. Wesley in his heart longed to have the faith that those Moravians had. (He never got it here in the States. Of course, it was a colony then.) He went back to Britain and went to a little meeting in Fleet Street at which a Moravian preacher was preaching. What do you think the Moravian preacher was reading? He was reading the preface to Romans by Martin Luther. As he heard that being read, John Wesley said, "I felt a strange warming in my heart. God had saved me."

So began the first great evangelical awakening in the British Isles. It was to spread to every part of Britain. John Wesley went everywhere. They turned him out of the churches, so he stood on the gravestones, on the tombs to preach to the people in the graveyard. Then they turned him out of the graveyard so he went to the fields. One time he preached to thirty thousand men who were considered to be the off scouring of society; they were all miners. He said, "You know I was so dead as I preached to them that I could not believe that anything was happening until I saw a strange sight. All of their faces were black and white stripes, and then I understood that they were weeping."

Thousands and thousands of people were saved all over Britain and in the States. Those early Methodists came over here, and before long George Whitfield, the other great colleague and companion in that move of God. Whitfield and the Wesleys fell out on the whole matter of predestination and split the move in two.

The Brethren

Almost a hundred years later, simultaneously in Dublin, Plymouth, Bath, and Bristol companies of people came together seeking simply to meet as Christians and believers without any regard for denomination. It was one of the most remarkable movements of the Spirit of God in the history of the church. It was the beginning of what we now call Brethrenism. It was to spread over the whole British Isles and far, far beyond, and to have an influence upon the things of God such as no other movement of the Spirit of God has had.

By the way, the Wesleyans gave us something else. The Puritans never accentuated new birth, but the Wesleyans emphasised being born again, and they gave us this truth, which has never again been taken away from us that we are to be born again. They gave us also something else—that there is an assurance of salvation to be had. There is an experience of the Spirit of God to be had.

The Brethren gave to us another wonderful truth—that all the people of God are one. We all belong to one another. They emphasized the coming of the Lord as no other group before them had done. Oh, the simple way in which they broke bread together, and they worshipped the Lord together, just giving over to the Spirit of God to lead whom He would in worship and praise and in serving the Lord together. Some of these features have been in the others by the way. The Wesleyans had class meetings in the early days where they used to meet together, and one would have a hymn, one would have a Scripture, one would have a testimony and one would pray as led by God. The Quakers also had these features in the beginning.

The Spirit of God recovered the unity of God's people through the Brethren and gave it to us in a way that has never been lost, at least to the true believer.

The Pentecostals

Then in 1906, we had the advent of Pentecostalism. Some people do not really recognise Pentecostalism as a move of God at all, but we have to. There has been a history written for the first time from the academic point of view of Pentecostalism, and when you really read it in a detached way, you have to recognise that God was in this thing. For God was telling us that the gifts of the Spirit are not lost; that they are present in the body of Christ, that there is an enduement with power from on high.

If we were to bring all these features together we would have fullness. The tragedy of the whole thing is that nearly every single one of these movements had major divisions within twenty years. Within fifteen years the Puritans divided into four. The Reformers, within a matter of twenty years, divided again into three major groups. The Quakers did not get divided, thank God, until much later. The Methodists divided within the first twenty years into two huge groups, Whitfield on one side, the Wesleys on the other. The Brethren within twenty years divided into Open Brethren and Exclusive Brethren. The Pentecostals were not going more than ten years before they divided into so many divisions it is impossible to enumerate. Isn't that amazing!

Modern Church History

Of course, since then there have been some remarkable things in modern history. We must mention what happened in China with our brother Watchman Nee. We must mention what happened in Britain with that prophet of God, Austin Sparks. I believe we are now in a move of God that we are being pushed into by political and economic pressures, behind which stands God. We are being pushed into a discovery of one another again. We are being pushed into fellowship with one another. We are being pushed into a grassroots participation. Everywhere I go now in universities everyone wants grassroots participation. The students want to take part; they want to be able to talk back and all the rest of it. So now at last something is happening in the church of God. The old pulpit/pew relationship appears to have gone forever; thank God, because something is happening. There would never have been a Reformation without economic and political pressures. God was behind them. Now, God has turned the tables around and is using something to push us back to finding one another in the Lord, moving together in the Lord, expressing our priesthood as believers in the Lord. As we come to the end of this age, however long this last phase will be, I do not believe that we can cut ourselves off from all that has gone before. It is a continuity. God forbid that any one of us could cut ourselves off from what God has done in the past. We belong to them and they belong to us.

Lessons from the Past

Finally, what are the lessons we learn from them? I shall enumerate them and not spend time on them. Here are the lessons. Within a generation, most movements of the Spirit of God have formalised and died and crystallised into institutions. In nearly all of them, within twenty years major divisions have resulted in the fragmentation of the whole. It is an interesting fact that God, who is absolutely sovereign, appears not to be bothered about keeping alive these things. Now this must be a question to all of you who are students of the Word. Why, if God is sovereign, does He not keep alive these things? It seems to me that once the first generation is over it is as if God says, "Now we will let that die." It is as if God gets in the first generation, and the second generation if they are in the good of the first, all the values He wants, and then He lets it die. In other words, it seems to me that the materials for the city of God are produced by the Spirit during the beginning of these movements and are never lost. In every single thing that God has ever done by His Spirit in the history of the church, it may seem that man has destroyed it. It has not been destroyed! God has caught it up to heaven; it is the man-child and has gone into heaven. The gold, the precious stones, the pearl of Christ's make up wrought in His people in the most difficult circumstances has gone into the city of God, and at the end you will find it there.

Sometimes people think what happened in China has all been lost. No, no, no! All the values of what God did in China are in the city, and in the end we shall find them there. In every single generation in the history of the church God has brought all that together. Recovery appears to be progressive. We find for instance, justification, the access of every redeemed child of God into the presence of God through the Lord Jesus, the Word of God as authoritative. We find independent congregations, eldership, baptism, the inward nature of everything in the church, new birth, oneness of the people of God, the gifts of the Spirit, enduement with power.

I wonder what God is trying to do in our day? I sometimes wonder if God is trying to reveal to us and finally recover the outward nature of the vessel that we might finally understand what kind of vessel it is that all of this is to be contained within. I do not know, but what I do know is that what has been recovered by the Spirit of God through the history of the church has never again been lost. In the real people of God in every generation those values live on. That is why I am so concerned and why I speak about this principle of continuity. Why should we cut ourselves off from it? Why must we impoverish ourselves as if it does not belong to us, as if it is just history. It is all ours, and we have something to add in our day and generation. May God make us faithful.

It seems to me that we have in this whole matter an illustration of the overcomer and the whole people of God. You will notice that once something has been lost, every time God recovers it, it is through that little remnant, that little minority amongst the people of God who have been prepared to lay down their lives and suffer whatever it is for the whole, not to be a superior, elite in a circle, but for the whole church of God. May the Lord teach us what it means to be an overcomer! That is, that in our day and generation we may be those who are prepared to go the whole way with the Lord whatever the price, whatever the cost, to lay down our lives so that all the people of God in our day and generation may benefit. May the Lord help us and keep us. Vision determines how long any move of the Spirit of God lasts. It is interesting that the Brethren have lasted in life the longest of many of these moves of God, because they saw something more than many others. May God make us people of vision, real vision, people who have an understanding of the will of God and an understanding of the purpose of God.

Shall we pray?

Dear Lord, help us to understand what has been said this evening. We are all in, as it were, this one thing that Thou hast been doing through this age. Help us to understand it and help us to draw from all those values the past recovered and deposited, as it were, in the life of Thy people. We do not want to do without any of them; we want these features to be found in our gatherings. We want somehow or other that all these things that have been so fragmented and isolated and sort of crystallised denominations, may somehow or other be brought together in a fullness, and that we may express, dear Lord, something of Thy full mind in these days in which we live. Only Thou can make this word this evening a living reality to us all. Do it, Lord. We ask it in the name of our Lord Jesus Christ. Amen.

4.
Principles of Fellowship–Authority

Ephesians 1:15–23

For this cause I also, having heard of the faith in the Lord Jesus which is among you, and the love which ye show toward all the saints, cease not to give thanks for you, making mention of you in my prayers; that the God of our Lord Jesus Christ, the Father of glory, may give unto you a spirit of wisdom and revelation in the knowledge of him; having the eyes of your heart enlightened, that ye may know what is the hope of his calling, what the riches of the glory of his inheritance in the saints, and what the exceeding greatness of his power to usward who believe, according to that working of the strength of his might which he wrought in Christ, when he raised him from the dead, and made him to sit at his right hand in the heavenly places, far above all rule, and authority, and power, and dominion, and every name that is named, not only in this world, but also in that which is to come: and he put all things in subjection under his feet, and *gave him to be head over all things for the church, which is his body, the fullness of him that filleth all in all.*

Two Extremes of Authority

I would like to take up another principle of fellowship, by the enabling grace of God, and it is the principle of authority. I have no doubt in my own heart that it is over this principle that the enemy is working so very strongly. On one hand we find gatherings where there is no authority at all and everybody does that which is right in his own eyes. It is a kind of free-for-all and our gatherings, especially what we call house fellowships, have become a kind of place where we are released from all responsibility, all limitation, and all discipline. They are just places where we sort of enjoy the Lord and, where in many ways, we are living in a fool's paradise. For instance, you can go into one of these house fellowships, and no one has to do any tidying up. No one from the general company does anything about putting out any books or seats. No one helps you at all in any way. You just come in. You just sit down. You just enjoy yourself. You don't have to take any responsibility. You do not necessarily have to be punctual; you can come at any time; just drift in and drift out. It is a kind of free-for-all, and in some cases it seems it has been almost reduced to a doctrine of freedom, as if this is what it means not to be under law but under grace.

Then of course, there is the other end of the line where we have such a recognition of authority and such an enforcement of authority that the whole thing becomes a hierarchy. We are bound to obey, and whatever the brother says, whoever it is, we have to do what he says. If we do not do what he says, we are ostracised and finally excluded from that company of believers.

In between there are a number of other varieties. Therefore, I believe this principle of authority in the matter of fellowship is vital. The first thing I would like to underline is the absolute headship of our Lord Jesus Christ. God has made the Lord Jesus absolute Head to the church.

The Absolute Headship of Christ

Ephesians 1:22, 23 says, "He put all things in subjection under His feet, and gave him (that is Christ) to be head over all things to the church, which is his body, the fullness of him that filleth all in all."

Colossians 1:18: "And he is the head of the body, the church: who is the beginning, the firstborn from the dead; that in all things he might have the preeminence."

No matter what the situation, no matter what the problems, no matter what the circumstances that we find ourselves in as the people of God, Christ has been made Head over all things to the church. God recognises no other head, and all substitutes for Christ's headship are a terrible evil.

Now let me make it quite clear here. We are not just talking about papacy or an episcopacy or some committee or council or goal. Most of us would probably feel that those are the kinds of things which get in the way of the headship of the Lord Jesus Christ. But you can have a New Testament pattern or a group of elders which appear to be as New Testament as you can get, but if those men substitute their heads, their wills, their brains, their intelligence for the headship of the Lord Jesus Christ, it is a pernicious evil!

That is why you sometimes find in New Testament companies, which appear to be really returning ostensibly and apparently to New Testament principles, the thing is dead. It is as formal and dead as anything institutional. Younger ones ask themselves, "How can we have a New Testament pattern and it be so dead? But I can go somewhere else which does not have a New Testament pattern and I find life?" Therefore, they come to the conclusion that God is not the least bit interested in any kind of pattern. This is wrong. There is a pattern, in one sense, and it is within the life of our Lord. Eldership, as such, is a principle because it is, as it were, the expression of the authority of our Lord Jesus Christ. But if those men put their heads in the place of the Lord Jesus Christ, that becomes a pernicious evil. It will effectively paralyze the work of God. It will, as it were, make that company of believers lifeless; it will formalise them.

It is a strange fact that you can have a committee of men who have been so dealt with by the Holy Spirit and are so dependent upon the Lord that the headship of Jesus Christ can come right through them. On the other hand, you can have a New Testament pattern where men have put their heads in the place of our Lord collectively or individually and destroy the flow of divine life.

Christ—Not a Figurehead

Christ is not a democratic monarchy. (I shall have to explain this being here in a republic.) He is not some kind of national figurehead. I come from a kingdom. I am a subject of the United Kingdom, and in one sense I suppose I am quite proud of that. I think you folks have done very well since you have seceded, but I think you might have done a good deal better if you had stayed with us. However, having said that on your bicentennial year, I have to tell you that I live in a kingdom which has a constitutional monarchy. What do I mean? The queen is a democratic monarch, a constitutional monarch. In other words, she does not, in actual fact, rule the country. The country is ruled by Parliament, but the queen signs everything and in that sense legalises everything. In other words, at the opening of Parliament the queen makes a speech to both the House of Lords and the House of Commons. She may say things like this, "I am going to nationalise the steel industry." She may be very much against the nationalisation of the steel industry, but she has to say it because her speech has been written by the party who has the majority, maybe by the Prime Minister or somebody else. She has to read it as if it is her speech. When the law is passed, it is taken to the palace for the queen's signature. When she has placed her signature on it, it becomes law. She is a national figurehead, and she unites the whole country above politics and which I think is a very good thing.

Now, what we have done with the Lord Jesus is to make Him a democratic monarch. We have made Him a constitutional monarch. We have made him a kind of national figurehead. We write His speeches and give them in His name. I think about ninety percent of the sermons preached have nothing whatsoever to do with our Lord Jesus Christ, in the sense, that they did not originate with Him, but they are spoken in His name. We write speeches for Him. We put ideas into His head. We pass laws in His name. We use His name for all kinds of teaching, and so on.

I sometimes put it like this—you know the kind of committee where we get together to discuss what we are going to do for the coming autumn, fall and winter. We say, "We are going to have a word of prayer. So and so will you lead us in prayer? We are going to seek the Lord now about the coming programmes." We all bow our heads, and the brother prays, "Oh Lord, do show us (all twelve of us) and reveal to us what is Thy programme for this coming fall and winter. Give us to know Thy will and Thy mind." Sometimes it is not quite as clear as that, but never mind. We ask Him and then we say, "... through our Lord Jesus Christ Amen."

Then whoever is leading the meeting says, "Now so and so, I believe you have the programme for this coming fall and winter; could we hear the bookings you have?" He says, "Yes, we have so and so booked, so and so booked, and so and so booked." Then there is a little bit of discussion as to whether we should modify this or adjust that or the other. Then at the end of it we bow our heads and say, "Now, thank you Lord for revealing your will to us." Then for the rest of the fall and winter we wonder why there is no blessing, why there is no abundant life, why the Lord does not seem to be committed to us. The fact is we are passing the law and we just want His signature. We don't expect Him to be an absolute monarch. We don't expect Him to direct us.

We don't expect Him to govern us. We just expect that we do all that in His name. We have made Him a constitutional monarch, but our Lord Jesus Christ is the practical and absolute Head of the church.

I suppose we have made every mistake it is possible to make in Richmond, England, but if we have gotten anywhere by the grace of God it has been simply because we were stupid enough and dumb enough to believe that what God says in His Book is absolute truth. If He says that Jesus has been made Head over all things to the church, Jesus is Head over all things to the church, and in the Head is the mind, the will, and the intelligence. Therefore, we recognised this one simple fact: if we were to get on our knees and really on every level of our life together ask the Lord, "What would You have us do? How would You have us do it? Shall we go this way? Or shall we go that way?" He would make known to us what is His mind.

We have found in our little experience that the Lord, if I may put it almost irreverently, has fallen over Himself to let us know His will and His mind. It is as if it is a rare thing for people to get on their knees and actually say, "Lord, You are our Leader; You are our Director; You are our Lord; You are our Head. Now lead us."

Just because people cannot see Him they seem to think, "Since we cannot see Him we better make this brother the head or that brother the head or these brethren the head. Let them put their heads together." We have this democratic idea that if you get a few heads together, you are bound to be safe. But you can have five heads put together, 20 heads, 100 heads, or God forbid, 1000 heads put together, and the whole lot can go off the rails.

The majority has rarely been right. Again and again and again, you will find that the minority has got the mind of the Lord. Haven't you found that some of you good Baptists? I remember some of those church meetings I used to be in where again and again the will of the Lord was out-voted by a vast majority. The idea was that if you had all those saved people together, the majority must be right; but they were not right. One thing after another was voted in by the majority, and I am talking about real believers, not just nominal Christians.

The fact of the matter is that in some very real way we have to recognise that Jesus Christ has been made Head over all things to the church. Our problem is that because we cannot see our Lord, because we cannot see, as it were, the Holy Spirit, we cannot put this into practice. We think it is being mystical. But do you know that on every single level of church life, whether it is children's work, or young people, or the whole church, or the practical side, the material side of things, or whether it is, as it were, spiritual policy, for want of a better word, if we would only get on our knees and ask the Lord for His mind, He would give it!

Now, there are times where we have to wait for the Lord's mind, and that is what we find so difficult. You see, if we felt we could say, "Lord, what shall we do about this?" and He immediately said, "Yes, do this and this," we would find that easy. But there are times when the Lord says nothing, and we have to wait and wait and wait. However, every time we have had to wait, we found that it had been abundantly justified in the end. There have been times when we have not waited but have gone ahead and we have fallen into tragedy. When the Word of God says that our Lord

Jesus Christ is Head of the church, it means precisely what it says. He *is* Head of the church!

Dear family of God, we have talked about the principle of continuity. The fact is that we are in something which God has been doing from the beginning of this age, and we all belong together with all that God has recovered as our heritage. We must not despise it, or devalue it, or reject it; not any single part of it. For if God is going to do anything in our day and generation, all the features that have been recovered in the history of the church will be found amongst us.

I want just to say that all revival and renewal has flowed from a recognition of the simple fact that the Lord Jesus is Head over his people. It is as simple as that. Every single movement of the Spirit of God in the history of the church has stemmed from the recognition on the part of a man or a few men or a company of people, of the absolute headship of Jesus Christ. It does not matter where you turn in the whole history of the church, every movement has begun with it. Every departure has stemmed from the rejection of the Lord Jesus as practical and absolute Head of the church, the substitution of the Lord Jesus as Head with other bodies or other sort of forms.

It seems such a simple thing. I was speaking to someone the other day who told me that before he was saved he found it the hardest thing in the world to kneel. He just could not kneel before the Lord. I think this finds an echo in many of our hearts, especially men. They find it so hard to bow before the Lord. But you know, when we are saved, we still seem to have this resistance when it comes to the government of the Lord. We find it hard to simply seek Him in prayer. It is much easier to spend an hour discussing and discussing opinions here, opinions there. We come in with this; we come in with that—this conception, that conception, this idea, that idea. It is much easier than to get on our knees and say: "Lord, we are putting aside all our opinions and conceptions, and we want You to direct us."

Now don't get me wrong; there may be a place for fellowship, but if only we began with a recognition of the headship of Jesus Christ instead of bringing in the headship of Jesus Christ after we have done all the talking. But that is what we do. We do all the talking and then we get on our knees and say, "Now Lord, You know; just show us." If only we would recognise Jesus as Head!

I wish that all our gatherings could begin that way. I think there comes a clarity into the gatherings of God's people when at the beginning of them, there is a simple recognition of the headship of Jesus Christ. I go into some places where the brethren do not even pray before a gathering. Everyone just drifts into it. No one gets into the secret place of the Lord beforehand and recognises Jesus Christ as Head and Lord over the gathering.

The Battle—Not Flesh and Blood

Do you understand that we are not wrestling against flesh and blood but against principalities and powers? If we just drift into this kind of thing we shall find that the enemy gets a foothold from the very beginning and the meeting begins in a kind of hard, heavy way, and only when we are just about to part do we get through. Do you know those kinds of meetings? About a quarter of an hour before we go home we find the sun has come out from the clouds; we feel as if the Lord is shining on us. All of that should be done at the beginning!

There should be brethren who get together before the Lord before any gathering and establish the fact that we are not subject to Satan, nor to any of these principalities and powers, these world-rulers of darkness, these hosts of wickedness. We are under the headship of Jesus Christ! We want to show the flag! In the good old days they used to send the gunboats up the river and show the flag. That was all that was needed. You do the same kind of thing over here. You have copied us no end, you Americans. You show the flag in different parts of the world. You know, send the 7th Fleet in or the 6th Fleet in.

I remember when there was trouble in the Middle East in the Mediterranean. (This is a digression and not spiritual at all.) There was civil war in Jordan, and all you did was send the U.S. 6th Fleet in, just cruised round like a pleasure tour. That finished the civil war in Jordan. Syria did not even bother to attack Jordan, which she was going to do. If she had attacked Jordan, Israel would have attacked also, but you showed the flag.

What we need to do is show the flag. At the very beginning of our times we should show the flag: "Jesus Christ is Lord of this company! We are His people and under His headship! We declare it! We confess it!" It is a simple recognition by which at the very beginning of our time we bow the knee and recognise Jesus as Lord and Head. Then, it is as if the Holy Spirit says, "Now I can commit Myself. You have made a simple recognition that is so childlike, but because you have made this recognition, all the anointing is yours, all the resources are yours, all the fullness is yours, all the covering is yours, and all the protection is yours!

If you do not make this recognition, then I have to leave it because it is as if you think you can get through this without Me." This is so when we have these times which we could call sort of business times, when we get together and we have to decide on policy or make decisions. Oh, if only instead of all this interminable discussion, which we call fellowship, we could first recognise the headship of Jesus Christ and recognise another simple thing: that we have no wisdom.

Years ago when I was first saved, I had a Swedish aunt who adopted me and my sister spiritually and looked after us, and from her we learned some of our first lessons. I remember that she used to say to me: "Now Lance, you make this your daily prayer. Take James, chapter 1:5-6, and say to the Lord: 'Lord, I stand on Your promise that says if any man lack wisdom let him ask of God who gives to all men liberally and upbraideth not; and it shall be given him. But let him ask in faith, nothing wavering.'" Every day for about six years I used to stand on that promise.

I think sometimes we get lazy after a while. We tend to think: "I know the Lord. I know something about the Bible. I'm a brother now, a responsible brother." So we do not feel the need to recognise that we have no wisdom. But if only at the beginning of our time we would say: "Lord, here we are. So and so has a degree, so and so is very clever about this, but we are so stupid when it comes to the things of Yourself. Lord, the more degrees we have the dumber we are when it comes to Thy work. Oh Lord, we cast ourselves upon thee. Be wisdom to us. Manifest Thyself as wisdom in us according to Thy promise." This is a simple recognition of Jesus Christ as Head.

The Reality and Practice of Fellowship

There is something I want to say further on this matter of fellowship. It is very, very much connected to the principle of authority. The reality of fellowship and the practice of fellowship flow from our connection to the Head. Now I cannot make a statement more important than that in this matter of fellowship. The reality of our fellowship and the practice of real fellowship flow from our direct connection to the Head.

What I mean is this. You all know this kind of thing where we all meet together, but there is nothing between us. We are all believers, we are all redeemed, we are all saved, and some of us really know the Lord, and some are choice saints; yet there is no connection. We all keep saying: "What is wrong? What is wrong? Here we are all sitting together and yet somehow we do not flow together. We are not being built together. We are not being fitly framed together. We are not somehow knit together. What is wrong?"

Some people make the great mistake of saying, "We have got to get closer to each other. Ah! We know what it is; we must have meals together." Some people will say, "No, we must live together. That is the way. If we all live together, we'll get closer together." Others will say, "We must pool our resources." Now, I am not saying that these things are necessarily wrong. The early church at Jerusalem did exactly that. They lived together in a community. They pooled all their money together. They ate together. Their whole life was completely shared. But it is an interesting fact that we have no other record of that happening again in the New Testament. Nevertheless, it was a valid experiment. It was an expression of fellowship in Jerusalem, but in Antioch they did not do that. As far as we can tell they evidently all had their own homes, but there was real fellowship. You will remember that the elders met together and fasted before the Lord, and it was during that time that the Lord said, "Separate Me Paul and Barnabas unto the work to which I have called them," (See Acts 13:2). My point is this: we have to be very livingly connected to the Head, not to one another firstly. Primarily, it is not to one another that we need the connection. Primarily, it is to the Head that we need the connection.

Hold Fast the Head

Colossians 2:19 says, "And not holding fast the Head, from whom all the body, being supplied and knit together through the joints and bands, increaseth with the increase of God."

Increasing with the increase of God is directly connected with holding fast the Head. Or again, "being supplied and knit together." Oh, don't we need a supply? Sometimes our fellowship gets into heavy weather, doesn't it? Clouds come and we make really heavy weather of it, and what we need is to hold fast the Head being supplied with grace, power, divine resources, and divine wisdom. "Being supplied and knit together through the joints and bands, increases with the increase of God."

Now this is the point: you make sure that your relationship with the Lord Jesus Christ as Head and Lord is absolutely clear, and you will find the body. Do not try to get a horizontal relationship first, but get the vertical relationship, and you will find the horizontal relationship.

Ephesians 4:15-16: "But speaking truth in love, may grow up in all things into him, who is the head, even Christ; from whom all the body fitly framed and knit together through that which every joint supplieth, according to the working in due measure of each several part, maketh the increase of the body unto the building up of itself in love."

"Grow up in all things into him who is the head, even Christ, from whom the whole body." I wish that this principle could be seen on every level of church life. I wish that all leadership could simply see that it is holding fast the Head that is so essential.

What problem do you have? Don't try to meet it with your own conceptions or even your biblical knowledge. Meet it by holding fast the Head. Are there problems between leaders? Meet those problems by holding fast the Head. If I hold fast the Head and you hold fast the Head, we will surely come together somehow. Whatever the problems are, whatever the differences of opinion, we will surely come together if you hold fast the Head and I hold fast the Head.

I wish this could be seen on every other level also. You may be the youngest person in the church, the youngest person in the company of believers. You have only just been saved. But if you will only learn from the very beginning to hold fast the Head and grow up in all things into Him as the Head, you will find your place in the body.

People often come to me and say they feel out of things. It's very interesting because sometimes I go to a company that has really gone places with the Lord, and then somebody whom I really feel knows the Lord comes up to me and says, "I feel so out of it." One of the most common things I find in going round is to find people who feel out of things. They are right in things ostensibly, but they feel out of it. The devil is the past master at telling us that we are not really in: "You are just nothing; you are not really in." The only answer to this is to resist the enemy by holding fast the Head and growing up into Him, as Head, in all things.

What does it mean to grow up into all things in Him as the Head in all things? That is an interesting thought, isn't it? Both the "holding fast" and the "apprehending the Head," is a very strong word. It is really taking hold of the Head. It is not that you just sort of drift into it, but you have to hold fast! Arrest the Head! Apprehend the Head! Take a firm hold on the Head!

Grow Up into the Head

Then it says, "Grow up in all things into Him as the Head." Isn't that interesting? That means that there are many problems, many circumstances, and many situations in which we have to learn to grow up into Christ as Head. We have got to discover His Lordship, discover His headship, discover His mind. We have to discover His will and do it! We have to grow up in all things into the Head. The oneness of the body—it's function, it's growth, it's increase—is all dependent upon the relation of members to the Head. If one member is out of gear with the Head that is an area of paralysis in the fellowship.

You see, we are talking about sharing Christ, but we share Christ as every one of us keeps in that direct relationship to our Lord as Head. When this principle is obeyed, then you find life and fullness of life. You find development and resurrection all the time. Every time you go into death you find that you come out into life, into resurrection. You find all these things as you obey this principle of the headship of the Lord Jesus. But when it is denied, even unwittingly denied, then immediately there is weakness, defeat, fragmentation, heaviness, and inhibition.

Many companies I go into seem to suffer from a permanent heaviness, and I sometimes wonder whether it does not go back to this non-recognition of the headship of the Lord Jesus Christ. Of course, these folks really do recognise the Lord Jesus as Head, but they do not declare it! They do not establish the fact! It is as if somehow or other they are a million miles away from the enemy and from the world that lies in the evil one. Whereas we are in a world that lies in the evil one. We are wrestling. That is not a polite sport like tennis or badminton. Wrestling is all sweat. Sometimes you get someone quite heavy and tough sitting on you, pinning you down to the ground! You have your arm twisted up your back or your leg getting pulled off. Some Christians seem to think that there is no such thing in the Christian life as that, but we wrestle not against flesh and blood but against principalities and powers.

There are times when we must expect the enemy to sit on us to get, as it were, our arm right up our back. We have got to learn how to get the victory even in such situations. This is not a tennis match where the enemy is over there and we are here, and someone is chalking up the marks. We are in something that can only be described as wrestling, and we need to declare that Jesus Christ is Lord and Head!

The Place of Man in the Matter of Headship

Now I would like to say something about the place of man in this because this is where we get a lot of our trouble. Let me say this straightaway: I have dwelt quite a lot on what some people would call the mystical side of things. I do not call it the mystical side at all because to me it is intensely practical. If our Lord Jesus Christ has been made Head over all things to the church, it is the simplest, most practical, most obvious, most rational, most logical thing to do to get on our knees and recognise Him on every level of our lives! Then we will see a life flowing through the church such as we have not seen for many, many years. We shall see the Lord beginning to qualify leadership, beginning to raise up ministries, beginning to gift people because he is Head of us! ! He is practically Head and not just a figurehead.

The other area in which our trouble lies, of course, is the place of man in the headship of the Lord Jesus Christ. What is this place? We have to say there is a place for man in the headship of Jesus Christ. There are those who are called elders. There are those who are called deacons. On a wider scale, there is apostolic ministry. Now of course, some people tell us there is no such thing as apostolic ministry. But when we look at the history of the church, we discover that in every single movement of the Spirit of God, whether they are called apostles or not, there are men who have a unique anointing.

One of our problems is that whenever we begin to get into trouble, we react against the trouble and go the other way. This is a danger. I could give you example after example from the history of the church where tragedy has resulted because of reaction.

Never ever build anything on reaction. Reactions are rarely right because when we see something wrong we react and tend to go the other way.

Let me give you one good example of this. Martin Luther went so far in his early years that it is almost incredible how far he went. For many years some of the letters of Martin Luther were suppressed because they dealt with the matter of baptism. In the last thirty or forty years those letters have been made public, in which Martin Luther writing to Phillip Melanchthon, said this to him: "We must seriously question the whole method of infant baptism. We must remain open to our Lord as to whether perhaps the New Testament teaches the baptism of believers."

He was also very, very deeply influenced by what were called the Bohemian Brethren. The Bohemian Brethren had a meeting together, which was as near to the New Testament norm as you could get. It was Martin Luther's vision that that should be, as it were, the kind of way that the believers who had been revived by the Spirit of God should gather together all over Europe. Then, what happened? A group of men calling themselves "The Prophets" began to make all kinds of predictions, and those of you who know history will remember that a whole town and area went over to those people. They practiced free love. They spoke in tongues. They prophesied. They did all kinds of weird things and got themselves into a terrible mess. Luther and the other reformers were so horrified that they reacted so strongly they went right back and never again were able to face any other thing in Scripture. The Reformation ended not with what the devil did through "The Prophets," but through the reaction of Martin Luther and the other reformers to what was wrong.

The devil froze him so that he withdrew back into the Catholic system and would not even think of baptism again.

I could give you example after example from the Wesleyan era and from other eras where the same thing has happened. Now we are in danger of the same thing again. We see things that have got truth in them, but truth carried to such an extent that it becomes false. We are in great danger that of throwing the baby out with the bathwater.

For instance, we see in many areas now this kind of idea of authority, which is not, in my estimation, genuine. It is the abuse of authority, and because of that we are getting so afraid that we react and react and react so that we can no longer think about it in the right way. We must be very, very careful here.

Apostles and Elders

Truth is truth! Just because the largest number of people who die accidentally died from food poisoning, we do not stop eating. We may be more careful about what we eat, but we do not give up eating. Just because divorce is growing and growing, we do not stop marrying people.

What is the place of man in all this? The Scripture says that the church is built on the foundation of the apostles and prophets. There is such a thing as apostolic authority, and there is such a thing as apostolic ministry. But nowhere in the whole Bible is it right for apostles to take churches into their hands to rule them with a rod of iron or to systematize and structure them so that somehow or other they are dependent upon that apostle. That is wrong! It is absolutely wrong!

There are other things we can say too of this place of man. It says quite clearly in Hebrews 13:17: "Obey them that have the rule over you, and submit to them: for they watch in behalf of your souls as they that shall give account, that they may do this with joy, and not with grief: for this were unprofitable for you." We are told that we are to obey those that have the rule over us. When God has raised up men who really are qualified by his Spirit as elders, as elder brethren, we are to obey them. We are to pray for them. We are to cover them in the name of the Lord, but we are to obey them. The authority of our Lord Jesus Christ is expressed at times through men and that's where we have our problem, isn't it?

I have here a blackboard, and I want to draw a very simple diagram on it, which may help some of you. There is a teaching, and I do not think it is necessarily wrong, that this whole matter of authority is like a pyramid. (We have this very much in Britain.) It is a pyramid. At the top in a local church you have the elders, at the bottom you have the church, and in the middle area of the pyramid you have the responsible ones. The idea is that the ordinary mass of the church, the members of the body of Christ, are at the bottom, the responsible ones are in the middle, and at the top are the elders. It is a pyramid. We are to obey those that have the rule over us. In many ways this is not wrong. There is very much in the Word of God about the authority of elders or the authority of those with apostolic ministry.

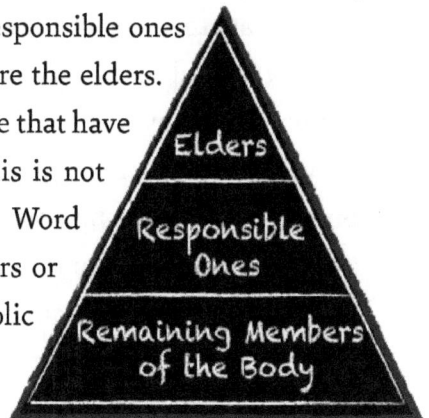

Elders

Responsible Ones

Remaining Members of the Body

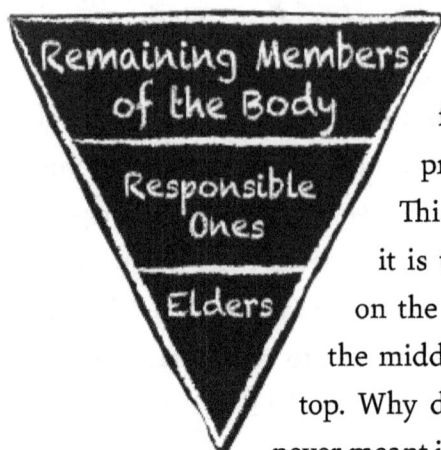

I like to put it another way, and I am very interested to find how violent a reaction this produces. Invert the pyramid. This is the way I put it, and I believe it is totally scriptural. The elders are on the bottom, the responsible ones in the middle, and the whole church on the top. Why do I do it that way? Elders were never meant just to be some kind of exhibition of authority. "You do what I say; I'm an elder. You just do what I say." The whole point of eldership is that they carry the whole burden and anguish of the church. This is the smallest point and can take the greatest weight. Is that biblical? It is absolutely biblical! How?

We read in 1 Peter 5:2, 3: "Tend the flock of God which is among you, exercising the oversight, not of constraint, but willingly, according to the will of God; nor yet for filthy lucre, but of a ready mind; neither as lording it over the charge allotted to you, but making yourselves ensamples to the flock."

Now again, here are the words of our Lord Jesus in Mark 10:42–45: "And Jesus called them to him, and saith unto them, Ye know that they who are accounted to rule over the Gentiles lord it over them; and their great ones exercise authority over them. But it is not so among you: but whosoever would become great among you, shall be your minister (your servant); and whosoever would be first among you, shall be servant of all (or slave of all). For the Son of man also came not to be ministered unto, but to minister, and to give his life a ransom for many."

What do these words of our Lord Jesus say? Simply this: if you and I would be elders or have any authority like this, we have got to be the slave of the whole church. It is interesting that the Lord used two words here. First, he used the word for a hired servant and secondly the word for a slave. A slave, of course, had no rights at all. He said, "Whosoever would become great among you shall be as your hired servant." This means that anyone in the church can say, 'Come" and you have got to come. You have got to serve them! You have got to be, in one sense, at their beck and call.

Then He says: "Whosoever would be first among you must be the slave." Even a hired servant has rights, but the slave has no rights at all. Whoever would be first must be slave.

The Principle of True Authority

Oh dear, dear family of God, if only this idea of authority had not been warped in our minds. Our idea of authority is of people who can walk around saying, "Do this," and you do it. "Do that," and you do it. You must obey me," and you must. If only we had seen that real authority was in our Lord Jesus Christ when He laid down His life for us and allowed the very creatures that He had created to nail Him to a tree that had been created by Him.

You see, our idea so often of royalty and kingship is pedigree, title, robes, and position—the mystique of royalty. The farther they are away from you, the more awesome and majestic they are; but our Lord Jesus was not like that. Do you know that when the Lord Jesus went from the garden of Gethsemane, they stripped him of his clothing? They stripped him naked. That shook all the mystique of royalty from him—the outward thing. They spat upon him. They pulled out the hair of his beard. They lacerated his back by scourging. They dressed him up in a captain's cloak and put a reed in His hand. They jammed the crown of thorns on His head and bowed before Him and said, "Hail, King of the Jews."

However, it was at that time when the Lord Jesus was stripped of all the paraphernalia of royalty, when He was stripped of all those kinds of things, which we tend to think make for royalty and majesty, that He was more royal than He had ever been before. For He revealed that His kingship is not built on position, or title, or clothing, or outward things, but it was built on an inner character. There was no crown that ever graced a monarch's brow more powerful than the crown of thorns. No sceptre in the hand of some great despot had ever been more powerful than the reed in the hands of the Lord Jesus Christ. He proved once and for all that He was worthy to be King of kings and Lord of lords. Anyone who can be stripped of all the mystique of royalty and come out as a King is worthy of the throne of God.

Now this is a kind of kingship you and I know nothing about. Some people seem to think that one day in the kingdom to come, we are all going to sit on golden thrones draped around the halls of heaven with sparkling diamonds on our hands and generally exhibiting ourselves as kings. As I have said before, God preserve us if some Christians ever get onto those thrones with the crabby little natures they have got. They have never allowed God to expand them or do any work in them. All they can do is hold on to position, hold on to title, hold on to the paraphernalia of office, because that is all they've got!

Kingship is not in outward things. It is in character! It is in life! It is in nature! Everyone who would come to the throne of God must go the way of the Lord Jesus Christ. There are times when we will be stripped of everything, when we will be ridiculed, derided, devalued. It is at those times that real kingship will be found in us.

No man ought to be an elder who is not prepared to lay down his life for the church. No man can be an apostle or in apostolic work or ministry who is not prepared to lay down his life for the Lord and for the people of God. We have no other safety, dear family! Otherwise we shall find that there will come into position, men who glory in their positions, who are building their own little empires, who are only interested in a kind of platform for themselves. So many of our companies, our house fellowships, can become platforms for little dictators. They could not get anywhere any other place, and so they come into their own little domain. May God preserve us from it all!

This is not meant in a harsh, critical, superior spirit. What I am saying is this: the principle of authority is not something with outward might and outward paraphernalia dependent on position and title. A man is qualified as an elder because he is able to let go of his name, of his reputation, of every single thing he has got and is prepared to become the slave of the whole church that the church might be built up. That is why I put them at the bottom. They take the whole weight upon themselves. They carry the whole church in their hearts. They have, as it were, everything weighing upon them.

Isn't this what the apostle Paul says in 1 Corinthians 4? He says in verses: 1, 9–13: "Let a man so account of us as of ministers of Christ, and stewards of the mysteries of God … For, I think, God hath set forth us the apostles last of all (last of all), as men doomed to death: for we are made a spectacle unto the world, both to angels and men. We are fools for Christ's sake, but ye are wise in Christ; we are weak, but ye are strong; ye have glory, but we have dishonor. Even unto this present hour we both hunger, and thirst, and are naked, and are buffeted, and have no certain dwelling-place; and we toil, working with our own hands: being reviled, we bless; being persecuted, we endure; being defamed, we entreat: we are made as the filth of the world, the off scouring of all things, even until now."

My dear friends, THAT is apostleship! If we were to have that kind of apostolic authority, O, God be blessed and praised! What a change there would be in the life of God's people! Here there is no empire building. Here there is no structuring of everything according to ourselves. Here there is no, as it were, setting forth of our own power and title and position. Here there are men who are prepared to die, doomed to death so that the church might know resurrection life. Here there are men who are prepared to fall into the ground and die so that there can be an abundant harvest, men who are prepared to lose their name that other names may be known everywhere, men who are prepared to die so that the body of the Lord Jesus Christ might be reproduced and built up all over the earth.

The Authority of the Lord Jesus

If you want to see this principle of authority, look at our Lord Jesus Christ. If you see in Him anything that is avaricious, anything that is selfishly aggressive, anything that is self-centered, I would like to know. The principle of authority is that a Man can be nailed to the cross by the very people He has come to serve, and in that moment have supreme authority. The principle of authority is that the very people He came to save can strip Him of every single thing that He had and do Him injury and despite, and at that moment He reigns supreme. That is spiritual authority.

Dear friends, THIS is the authority we need. We do not want this worldly authority. We do not want this thing that belongs to that world of pomp, and show, and position and title. Jesus said, "You shall not be called rabbi; you shall not be called master; you shall not be called father, for you are all brethren and you have only one Father and Master," (see Matthew 23:8–9). We need this authority. This is not just something that is a luxury; this is a principle. Without it fellowship will fragment, and without it there will be just a dissipation of all the values of the finished work of our Lord Jesus Christ.

I have spoken about the place of man in the headship of Jesus Christ. I would lastly just like to say what wonderful consequences there are when the authority of Christ is present. When the headship of Christ is a living practical reality and there is real fellowship amongst a company of God's people, there are some marvellous consequences! It is so simple really. *The* great result is that the authority of the risen, glorified Head of the church is manifested on earth. He is Head over all things to the church which is his body.

In II Corinthians 10:3–5: "For though we walk in the flesh, we do not war according to the flesh (for the weapons of our warfare are not of the flesh, but mighty before God to the casting down of strongholds), casting down imaginations, and every high thing that is exalted against the knowledge of God, and bringing every thought into captivity to the obedience of Christ."

Oh, to know such an authority! Oh that we, as the people of God, whether we are in Richmond or Raleigh or Glassboro or wherever else you come from, may know the manifestation of the authority of our risen Head in our midst.

There are strongholds, if you like emphasis, strong points of Satan in our areas and we will never know any relief until those things are cast down. There are imaginations which hold people in their grip and bondage, high things exalted against the knowledge of God. What are these ideologies? They are high things exalted against the knowledge of God.

Thoughts! Every single thing begins with a thought. Communism. Marxism began with a thought in the head of Karl Marx. Maoism began with thoughts in the head of Chairman Mao. Oh, if only the church could have taken those thoughts at their very beginning into captivity to the obedience of Christ. It does not mean that those people are necessarily saved, but we can take the thoughts captive because of the position of the church.

Oh, dear child of God, if only we, the people of God, were in the position we ought to be! If only we had dominion! If only we were exercising authority! If only we were reigning as kings on the earth, wouldn't it be wonderful?

God has given us keys. Keys are not ornaments; keys are power, authority. I have a little key here. Some of you have trouble getting in and out of your doors, but normally speaking, with just a little piece of metal, you don't even think about it. You just go up to the door, put in the key and go through it. I know people who go to the door, and they are all the time talking as they just put the little bit of metal in the hole, and they are in. You only ever think about keys when you have lost them. You go to the car, open it, get in, and in a few moments you have driven away. It is only when you have lost the keys that you have problems.

God has given the church the keys of the kingdom of heaven. "Whatsoever we bind on earth is bound in heaven, and whatsoever we loose on earth is loosed in heaven" (see Matthew 16:19). That is the principle of authority. Oh, that God would work such a fellowship in the hearts of us all that we might know something of this principle of authority.

Shall we pray?

Lord, we bow here before Thee, and we do pray together that somehow thou wouldst reveal to us this matter of authority. Thou seest all the many things that are happening all over the world in connection with the authority of our Lord Jesus Christ. Of one thing we are clear, Father, that Thou hast made our Lord Jesus Head over all things to us, the church. We recognise that glorious fact and confess that He is our Head. Oh, beloved Lord, we pray that Thou wouldst burn this truth into our hearts by Thy Spirit. Give us a clarity over it; give us a directness over it that we have never had before. Help us to hold fast the Head and thus discover the body. Help us to grow up in all things into Him as the Head, so that we may know the body building up itself in love.

Oh Father, we pray that Thou wouldst clear up all these ideas of man's place in the headship of the Lord Jesus Christ. Give us men who are selfless, men who are crucified, men who know the power and the fullness and anointing of the Holy Spirit. Give us such men as leaders, Lord, we pray. Oh, our beloved Head, let the word go out for the raising up of such men who shall be ensamples to the whole flock of God. Lord, raise up men with apostolic ministry and authority, men who lay down their lives that Thy Word may go forward in this world. Oh Father, hear us! We give it over to Thee! Thou knowest, Lord, that I have talked about this matter of authority in my childish way. But oh God, use the words that Thou hast enabled me to say by Thy Spirit to burn this matter into every heart that we may be those who really do follow the Lamb whithersoever He goeth. We ask it in His name. Amen.

5.
Principles of Fellowship–the Organic

Romans 12:1–16

I beseech you therefore, brethren, by the mercies of God, to present your bodies a living sacrifice, holy, acceptable to God, which is your spiritual service. And be not fashioned according to this world: but be ye transformed by the renewing of your mind, that ye may prove what is the good and acceptable and perfect will of God.

For I say, through the grace that was given me, to every man that is among you, not to think of himself more highly than he ought to think; but so to think as to think soberly, according as God hath dealt to each man a measure of faith. For even as we have many members in one body, and all the members have not the same office: so we, who are many, are one body in Christ, and severally members one of another. And having gifts differing according to the grace that was given to us, whether prophecy, let us prophesy according to the proportion of our faith; or ministry, let us give ourselves to our ministry;

or he that teacheth, to his teaching; or he that exhorteth, to his exhorting: he that giveth, let him do it with liberality; he that ruleth, with diligence; he that showeth mercy, with cheerfulness.

Let love be without hypocrisy. Abhor that which is evil; cleave to that which is good. In love of the brethren be tenderly affectioned one to another; in honor preferring one another; in diligence not slothful; fervent in spirit; serving the Lord; rejoicing in hope; patient in tribulation; continuing stedfastly in prayer; communicating to the necessities of the saints; given to hospitality. Bless them that persecute you; bless, and curse not. Rejoice with them that rejoice; weep with them that weep. Be of the same mind one toward another. Set not your mind on high things, but condescend to things that are lowly. Be not wise in your own conceits.

Could we have a further word of prayer?

Lord, we just want to bow again in Thy presence and recognise that both speaker and hearer are bankrupt to Thy grace. We are not going to get anything, Lord, out of this time except by Thy Spirit. We praise Thee, Lord; Thou hast made the provision for us in and through our Lord Jesus. Oh Father, we come on no other foundation, no other basis or ground than that which Thou hast given us—our Lord Jesus Christ and His finished work. Father, we ask Thee now if Thou wilt flood this time as we turn to Thy Word with divine light and divine life. Wilt Thou, we pray dear Lord, get this burden out of Thy heart and into our hearts. Oh, Thou seest the poorness of the vessel through which Thou must speak, but overcome all that we pray as we turn to Thee and let Thy strength and power be manifested in human weakness. Lord, Thou seest the weakness of our hearing. Let Thy power and strength be manifested there too, and let this whole evening rebound to Thy glory and honour because of Thy coming in through our Lord Jesus Christ. We ask it in His name. Amen.

As the Lord has enabled me I have been dealing with different principles of fellowship, and now I want to take another principle. I consider it to be as vital and strategic and important as any of the ones that we have thus far dealt with. It is the principle of the organic. I think this is another principle of fellowship that the enemy has used every device known to him and every weapon in his armory to somehow or other induce the people of God to contradict. He knows far better, unfortunately, than most of us that this principle is so vital to the building up of the body of our Lord Jesus Christ. It is so vital to real fellowship in practice that he will do anything and everything to blind the people of God to this matter. Ignorance of this principle in its practical outworking and meaning has led to many, many tragedies. We could spend the whole evening dealing with the tragedies in the history of the church. Not only that, but even in our contemporary situation we see things all over the world, which I believe began with the Spirit of God and seemed to be very much of the Lord at the beginning, contradicting this principle of the organic and producing a structure and a system which proved later to be abhorrent to the life of God. It is an imposition upon the life of the people of God, upon the life of Christ in the people of God, and therefore in the end becomes the very undoing of the deepest desire of the people of God. Some of these dear ones in these moves of the Spirit of God desire more than anything else to see the house of God built. They desire more than anything else to see the recovery of truth concerning the body of the Lord Jesus Christ. However, they themselves, through contradicting or contravening the principle of the organic undo the very thing that they long to see fulfilled in our day and generation.

The apostle Paul once said to the people of God at Corinth: "We are not ignorant of Satan's devices" (see II Corinthians 2:11). We must say sadly against ourselves that for the most part we are ignorant of Satan's devices. Oh, that the Holy Spirit could take something of this matter, this principle of the organic, and get it into our hearts. Oh, that somehow or other I might be enabled by the Spirit of God so to elucidate this principle, so to set it forth that the youngest of us here may see it. May the Lord help us.

The Organic Nature of True Fellowship

True fellowship is organic in its nature. You cannot structure it. You cannot systemize it. You cannot reduce it to a technique, to a matter of methods or regulations. You all know those sticky times that we can have when we suddenly say that this is the technique for fellowship. We do not put it quite like that, but we say, "We are going to have a time of fellowship." We sit ourselves around in a circle all looking at one another, and we say, "Now, this is how you have fellowship: one, two, three, and four, and the time becomes so sticky. We all look at each other and we look at the ground or we look at the ceiling, and we look over here and then over there. Then we look at each other, and we are so thankful when anyone even makes a peep. "Ahh! Someone is saying something." But even when they have said it, it is artificial. Then as soon as it is all over, we go out and we have fellowship. We make this mistake again and again. Now don't get me wrong. We do have times of real fellowship and they are the most blessed times. But when you try to structure this matter of fellowship, when you try to define methods of fellowship, techniques in fellowship, when you try to systematize it, you have somehow or other missed the whole point of real fellowship. Real fellowship is organic. It is something within the very life of God. Fellowship is inherent within the life of God.

When real spiritual life comes into a human being, they suddenly desire fellowship. It is the natural desire to find someone else who has got the same life, someone else who knows the same Lord, someone else who has been saved by the same Saviour. We long for fellowship, and the more life we have in us the more we feel our need of each other. The strange thing about the life of God is that it never makes us self-sufficient. Knowledge always makes us self-sufficient. We feel that the more we know in the head, the more we can do without other people, the more self-contained, and self-sufficient we can become. But the life of God somehow creates within us a hunger for the rest of the people of God. It creates within us a hunger for one another. It creates within us a sense of the need to share with others.

Organic Fellowship in the Body of Christ

Our Lord Jesus explained it in such simple ways. In one way He did not explain it. It was in His prayer, as He was speaking to His Father in John 17:21. But it is explained in those wonderful words of His: "That they may all be one, even as thou Father art in me and I in thee, that they may also be in us." That is organic! That is an organic fellowship. You cannot structure it or systematize it; you cannot reduce it to methods or techniques. That is a matter of life.

You have the same thing again in Romans 12:4–6: "For even as we have many members in one body, and all the members have not the same office: so we, who are many, are one body in Christ, and severally members one of another. And having gifts differing according to the grace that was given to us, whether prophecy, let us prophesy according to the proportion of our faith; or ministry, let us give ourselves to our ministry; or he that teacheth, to his teaching ..."

Suddenly we discover that this whole matter of being in Christ of being one body in Christ, of being members of Christ and members one of another is a matter of fellowship. We do not all have the same things. We have differing gifts according to the grace that was given to us. One has something, one has another and fellowship flows out of that; it is something organic.

The church, the body of our Lord Jesus Christ is an organism; it is organic in nature. Most evangelicals give lip service to this. Most theological seminaries and Bible colleges will teach that the church of the Lord Jesus Christ is a living organism, and then they teach everybody how to organise the organism. You will go to many, many believing, fundamental Bible colleges and seminaries, where you still find them, and you will discover they teach that the church is a living organism. Some, it is true, make a distinction between what they call the mystical body of Christ and the church on earth. This is a difference made between something which is all up there in the air in the heavenlies, invisible, intangible, universal, spiritual, and what is down here on earth which is organised, institutional, earthly, and has every kind of contradiction within it. There is this kind of teaching, which I must say I cannot find in the New Testament, that somehow or other up there we have the mystical body of Christ, and down here we have something institutional and organised. The fact of the matter is that if you take your New Testament and shut out all the ideas you have ever had about church, churches, and so on, you must come to the conclusion that the Word of God teaches us that the church on earth is the expression of the true church. Really all it is saying is that somewhere on earth is found a fellowship produced from heaven, governed by heaven, developed from heaven, which one day will be caught up to heaven and will return to the earth from heaven. You come to that conclusion.

An Organism vs. an Organisation

In these days in which we are living, thank God, more and more true believers are beginning to see the evil of denominationalism. Twenty years ago it was still very respectable to be denominational. Now, even if you are in a denominational church it is not so respectable to be denominational. We have to thank the World

Council of Churches for that and also the Second Vatican Council, as well as the fact that evangelicals are being pressurised into a corner where they are having to rethink the whole term "church." We find all over the place that suddenly it is respectable to be non-denominational. Even if you go to a Baptist Church it is acceptable to be non-denominational. Even if you go to a Methodist Church it is acceptable to be non-denominational. We even have groups who seem to feel that the main thing is to be non-denominational.

Denominationalism is not the disease. Listen carefully to me. Denominationalism is the symptom. You can get rid of every trace of denominationalism, and you have got rid of the symptoms, but the disease is still there. Sometimes (and this is not devaluing doctors) you can go to the doctor with some pimples or a rash. He is a very busy man, especially on our side of the Atlantic, and he says, "Yes, yes, here you are. Take this prescription and go." Off you go to the clinic and get something for it; you slap it on the rash, and it is gone. Then it comes out in another place, and you put it there, and it comes out again. We put it on there, and then it comes up somewhere else. The fact of the matter is that you can get rid of the symptoms, but the disease may stay inside you. To get rid of denominationalism, thank God, is a major step forward, but it is still only getting rid of the symptoms. What is the disease? The disease is organisationalism. You will discover that every single major denomination began as something organic. It became organised and structured outside of the life of Christ, and finally that has been crystallised into a denomination. The disease is organisationalism. Denominationalism, our labelling of ourselves by all the various names we have, is only a symptom.

What is the difference between an organism and an organisation? An organism often has got a very complex and intricate organisation. Don't make any mistake about this. An organism is thoroughly organised, but the difference between an organisation and an organism is that an organisation is static and man-made. It is put together from without to within, whereas an organism has to be born and it is within the life. For instance, my body is an organism. Every one of you here has a body. This is a remarkable fact, but every one of you has brought your body along with you. I am thankful for that. Now you have the illustration of this whole matter sitting with you. You are sitting in an organism and the organism is sitting in a chair. This organism, this body is an incredible thing, isn't it?

Organisation in the Physical Body

Quite a few years ago I was born. I was no more than the size of a baby, and everything that I have, except these clothes, has come out of that. How did I get like this? Did my parents stretch me? What did they do? How did it happen? I grew. You know that this body of mine has the most incredible organisation. I have got a central intelligence system, believe it or believe it not, and so have you. That intelligence system in you is more intricate than anything in the Pentagon and far more accurate. You have a telephone exchange, and all kinds of things in your body. Do you know that you have a built-in thermostatic control? When it gets too cold, you shiver. That is your thermostat at work. It says, "Now generate a bit of heat," and you start to shake. When you get too hot, you perspire, not sweat; you perspire.

That is the way your body is trying to cool you down. Where did it come from, this intelligence system in your body which is so remarkable and so accurate? Where did all this come from? Did it come from reading books? No! Did your parents endlessly play a kind of type to you that told you how you should react and the way you should react? No! You have the whole thing in your life, and it was all there when you were born. Parts of it were there but not developed because you did not need it, but as you grew the whole organisation that you needed developed so that you could be a contemporary human being. The whole organisation developed with you so that an organism is always contemporary. It never falls behind; it is always contemporary.

Here I am quite a few years after I was born, but I am contemporary. You may not feel it, but I am contemporary. In other words, my body is absolutely contemporary. I am not living back in 1935; I am living here in 1975. I have a body that is absolutely renewed. All the cells in my body are being renewed all the time. I am living a contemporary life. I have a contemporary body; I have a contemporary organisation. Some things have had to be cut back because I have grown older and other things have had to be developed in order to keep me contemporary. Now that is the difference between an organisation and an organism. An organisation is something which is put together; it never grows unless men change it from without. The only way you can bring an organisation, say from 1935, up to date is to change it from without. It does not grow from within. If you have a 1935 automobile it would still be a 1935 car in 1975. It is an organisation but it is a static organisation. However, my body is contemporary in 1975. How come? Because my body has an organisation that is developed from its life.

Now the whole key to this matter of organisation is where it finds its origin. In other words, we cannot do without organisation. It is stupid to think that the people of God can do without all organisation. Things must be done decently and in order. There must be a certain amount of organisation; that is obvious. But where does it come from? Does it find its origin in the life of God? Or is it something that we are thinking up and conceiving from the Bible and imposing upon the life of God?

Man-made Structure vs. Life

Sometimes we think that we see a weakness. Oh, I could speak for an hour on this matter just from observation and experiences I have had in all kinds of things all over the place. People see a weakness amongst the people of God and it is a real weakness. Then they begin to talk and discuss and think and think and think and discuss more. Then they look at the Bible and think again and discuss more. Perhaps at the end there is a little bit of prayer. Then they produce something to answer to the weakness. Of course, when it first comes in, it seems to be marvelous, absolutely marvelous. It seems to be an answer to the weakness, but what we have done unwittingly is build a structure that has not come out of the life. It has come out of our heads. And in the end that structure will kill the life of God inside. It will suffocate it. It will strangle it. It will bleed it to death like a parasite living on something else. It will drain everything out of it until it kills it.

Now that leads me to say that everything is within the life of Christ. The church is within the life of Christ. You cannot put the church together. That is the whole danger of books which define church principles to us. We need to see clearly what these things are, but the danger has always been the same. As soon as some people get hold of it, they are off. Now we have it! Now we can put it together. Just get a few people who love God together, and we will have this, and we will have that, and we will have the other. You here in America are terrific at this, but we are much more slow and stupid on our side of the Atlantic. Over here you have a business instinct. As soon as you see the technique or the way or the idea, boom, you are into it. That is the whole danger of this matter. We tend to think that anyone who is saved can put the church together, that somehow or other all you have to do is know certain teachings, certain principles and then you can begin. But principles are living things. They are within life. What we must do is recognise the principle and then see that we obey it. That is a different thing than trying to structure it.

What is the meaning of Pentecost? Don't you think those one hundred and twenty in the upper room, those dear ones, had a perfect church? There were one hundred and twenty saved believers in an upper room gathered around the risen Christ with an open Bible and pure doctrine. We could not have asked for more. But something happened on the day of Pentecost which was altogether in a different realm.

When the Holy Spirit came, what was the meaning of His coming? Is it that we might speak in tongues, that we might have gifts, that we might have a manifestation of the Spirit? My dear friends, all these things may be true, but that is not the meaning of the coming of the Holy Spirit. Those are the evidences or the equipment. What is the end? The end was that within the life of our risen Lord transmitted to us through the Holy Spirit, we suddenly find the church has come. In other words, it was the risen life of our glorified Lord that came by the Holy Spirit into one hundred and twenty members of a congregation and turned them into one hundred and twenty members of a body. From then on they were an integral part of one another. They belonged to Christ and to one another. They shared in a way they had never shared before. Now they were in living touch with the Head. Now they could get a direction from the Head. Slowly but surely an organisation began to develop, but it is interesting when you see the kind of organisation that developed and how it developed. It all came from the life of God.

In other words, it was fellowship that came with the Holy Spirit. "God is faithful through whom ye were called into the fellowship of His Son Jesus Christ our Lord," (1 Corinthians 1:9). The pattern of the church, the gifts necessary for the building up of the church, the functions of the body, are all within this life of Christ. Once we can see the life of Christ flowing through members of the body, we begin to see the development of a pattern.

People get so caught up on this thing about elders and deacons. All over the place they are caught up with this shepherding business, and everything else—we must have elders, we must have shepherds, we must have this, we must have that. My dear, dear friend, the first thing we need to bother about is loving one another, caring for one another. As we share that life and really submit one to another, God by His Spirit raises up those that must take responsibility amongst them, and we shall all know that they are the ones. There will be no question about it.

The tragedy is this: you can start making people elders who are not elders. You start making people deacons who are not deacons. You start making people apostles who are not apostles. I have people coming to us saying, "I am an apostle." God help us! They say, "I am an apostle." Really? They say, "Yes, yes. So and so laid his hands on me and set me aside, and I am an apostle." I have no doubt that there are times when hands should be laid on people and people should be recognised. But no wonder the apostle Paul said, "Lay hands on no man suddenly." Give time for the organic so that we can see in men something happening.

Oh, there is a pattern. Make no mistake about it. There is a church pattern. People always say that the Methodist pattern is found in the Bible, and the Baptist pattern is found in the Bible, and the Presbyterian pattern is found in the Bible, and the Episcopalian pattern, and the Brethren pattern, and the Pentecostal pattern. All these patterns are found in the Bible. Incredible isn't it? I am quite sure that our Lord, who was not limited in knowledge in any way, could have cleared this whole matter up by giving us one simple chapter in the New Testament which dealt exclusively with the pattern of the church once and for all, but He never did. That is why you get one pattern built on one thing and another pattern built on another and another pattern built on another, and they are all fragments of the pattern. Why? Don't you think our Lord, if He was so interested in the building of the church, could have made this whole thing clear to us? Of course, He could have! But what our Lord was trying to tell us was that the whole thing is a spiritual matter. It is within life, and the things of God are about His life, the resurrection life of Christ in at least two or more members of Christ. When we start to bother about that, then in the end the pattern will develop.

The Daffodil and the Onion

I have said this before, but I will say it again because it must be said again and again. You know, if you take a daffodil bulb and an onion bulb, they look so alike. How come that when I plant an onion bulb and a daffodil bulb, the daffodil comes up a daffodil and the onion an onion? Now wouldn't you think that sometimes they might make a mistake and the onion become a daffodil and the daffodil an onion? They look so alike. If they look so alike how come they never change or swap? Do you know you can take one daffodil bulb and plant it in a field of one million onions and the one million onions will come up onions and the one single little daffodil all on its lonesome in the centre of a field will come up a daffodil? Wouldn't you think that one bulb, which looks so much like those million onions would think: "I am so much like them, I will be an onion"? What is the key to the whole thing? The key is that the daffodil has a pattern within its life. It has daffodil life. The onion has an onion life. The pattern is in the life. Once the life starts to develop and grow you have the pattern.

We learned this lesson at home so deeply and so bitterly. When we first began years ago, we were as green as green can be. The one thing we did was to seek the Lord about everything, but on this matter we naturally were very taken by the fact of Scripture. We began to ask the Lord about elders and deacons because we saw in the Bible that there were such things as elders and deacons. As we sought the Lord we saw that they prayed and fasted. So we had two weeks of prayer and fasting. At the end of those two weeks of prayer and fasting, three men were made elders and four men were made deacons. We could not have had a more perfect church pattern, nor could we have gotten this pattern in a more spiritual way. After all, there are not that many people who would fast and pray for two weeks. Nevertheless, we prayed and fasted for two weeks, and we ended up with three elders and four deacons. Everything went on for a year or two blissfully. People were saved; everything seemed to be right and good.

Then after a year or two, we became aware, I, along with one or two others, of a kind of tremor, a kind of spiritual shaking deep down within the very life of the company of God's people. It ended one autumn with thirteen of us brothers, spending a day of fasting and prayer together to seek the Lord. It was in the study at Halford House, and I had my eyes open in prayer. As I looked across, I happened to see an acorn vase on the table. I always have difficulty in explaining this, but it was one of those little vases that you put an acorn from an oak tree in and you can see it grow. You see the roots come, and then you see the thing go out and grow up, and so on. As I was looking at it, the Lord said to me, "That is the answer to your prayer." So I looked again at the acorn vase and thought, I am crazy. Again the voice deep in me said, "That is the answer to your prayer." So I looked again at the acorn vase, and then the Lord said, "Do you see the acorn? The pattern you have got is like that outward shell, perfect, but it is static. Inside that acorn is life, and that life has the pattern of an oak tree in it. That life inside, if you will let it, will break the outward shell and grow up into an oak tree capable of reproducing other oak trees. I saw it in an instant! We had produced by the most spiritual means possible—fasting and prayer—a pattern. We did not know what to do. I shared it with the brothers, and we all prayed about it. We became of one mind and we sought the Lord: "What shall we do about this pattern that we have got?" We felt the right thing to do was to hand the whole thing over to God, which we did.

There came this wonderful Sunday when one after another all those with responsibility sort of faded out. The girl playing the piano sort of played something that sounded like a cross between a cat-fight and Arabic music. She tried again and it was worse, and then she finished altogether. We sang and she said she could not play anymore. That was her—out. One of the brothers who had quite a gift of the gab stood up, and what came out of him was neither a tongue nor was it English. It was certainly not grammatical. He stopped and started again. Then covering his confusion, he sat down and that was him—out. We ended that Sunday with one elder and one deacon, and then we said that it was no longer a New Testament pattern. So the whole thing went overboard and we all became brethren.

The most amazing thing happened. When we all became brothers again and just submitted ourselves to one another in the Lord, then the Lord started to do some quite remarkable things. People we least expected began to emerge in the next year heads and shoulders above the rest. The point was that the pattern we had was stopping the organic development and that thing was growing. You see, we are not dealing with something that is just a fairy tale. We are dealing with reality. This thing was growing inside the company. It was the organic life of Christ that had come up against the outward shell and it could not get through it. We had imposed the structure and the only way it could come through was by breaking the whole thing open.

I have seen more works that I believe were in their beginnings of God, wrecked by this elder, deacon, shepherding complex than anything else. You can make people elders; it is very hard to de-elderize them. The thing sort of gets right into our lifeblood. My point is simply this, that within the life of Christ you have all the pattern of the church. Once we bother ourselves about seeing that that life of the Lord Jesus is flowing through us, the pattern will come and so will the functions and so will the gifts. As we hold fast the Head by the Holy Spirit we shall find the body, and the body will increase with the increase of God. The body will build up itself in love. All these functions and gifts that are necessary will come.

Dealing with Weaknesses

There have been times when we have become deeply bothered in the work at home about certain weaknesses. By the grace of God He has stopped us every time from structuring something or systematizing something or somehow or other covering countering that weakness. What we have done instead is to have a week of prayer. We have been very honest with the whole company and said that we would have a whole day of prayer and fasting or we would have a week of prayer. We will tell the Lord that there is a weakness. For instance, take the matter of relatedness. We feel there is a lack in our company of discipline or relatedness at some particular point. We saw it as brethren. Then we said to the company that we feel the need to get before the Lord: "Lord, do something about this weakness amongst us." God has preserved us from somehow or other trying to answer those weaknesses with our own spiritual, Biblical solution. Instead, we have seen something and the Spirit of God come in and relate people to one another.

It all goes back to this whole thing of who is Head? It all comes to this principle of authority. If once we really see that He has been made Head over all things to the church, then when we see weaknesses, we shall get through to the Head and say to the Head: "Now Lord, we believe this and this and this needs to be done. Oh, release something from heaven. Do something about this matter."

Wouldn't we have been saved from some innovation, some things that have destroyed real works of God, if instead of just trying to answer some dullness in our meetings, or some dearth or some lack of ministry in our meetings, we had gotten on our knees and asked the Lord to do something? The Lord said, "Pray the Lord of the harvest." That is the principle—that He might send forth labourers into the harvest. If we see there is a need of ministry amongst us, why don't we get on our knees and say, "Lord, Lord, would you tackle whatever it is that is stopping You from raising ministry amongst us? Get through to it, Lord." By our very act of being together in the Lord and praying together, we find each other in the Lord. This is real fellowship. The Head has transmitted by the Spirit a sense of weakness to us. We begin to see an area of weakness and instead of trying to answer it, we go back to the Head and say, "What will You have us do?

There is a pain here. There is an area of paralysis here in the body. What would You have us do?" The Head always has an answer. Sometimes it is just to wait and He will work. Sometimes it is to take some kind of action, which He will show us; but oh, do you begin to understand my point?

People come to me and ask me if I am a Charismatic. I say dogmatically, "I am certainly a Charismatic." I want to know what they mean by Charismatic. They normally mean, do you speak in a tongue? But I say that the Scripture says quite clearly in Romans 6:23: "The wages of sin is death, but the *charisma* of God is eternal life in Christ Jesus our Lord." All the gifts are in the life of our Lord. Everyone who is born of God must be a Charismatic. So forget this business about the Charismatic. We are all Charismatics. What some of us may need is for the Holy Spirit to come upon us and be the dynamic for the gift so what is inside the life will come out.

The word for spiritual gifts of course is *pneumatic*. In 1 Corinthians 12:1 I have often wondered what would have happened if we had all been called Pneumatics instead of Charismatics. Someone says, "Are you a Pneumatic?" I am! I am a Charismatic. I am a Pneumatic. I am a Calvinist. I am a Pentecostal Plymouth brother. I am a Baptist with Lutheran conceptions and a Calvinist who sometimes sees the need of human responsibility. Well, forget that. I am a believer, aren't you? If we are in the body of our Lord Jesus Christ, then we shall find all these various emphases, won't we? They are too much for me. I cannot contain them within myself really. All I can do is be what God has made me in Christ, and all you can do is be what God has made you in Christ. But when we come together, we have a fullness.

Oh, may God help us in this matter of gifts. We need them! We need them! We need the gift of faith. We need words of wisdom and knowledge. We need the discerning of spirits. We need prophecy. We need these things. We desperately need the manifestation of the Spirit, especially when we go further and further into this last phase of world history. Without the life of Christ we cannot have the organic. You can have organisation; but without the life of Christ it is impossible to have the organic.

The Cross and Resurrection Life

Now that leads me to say this. There can be no resurrection life without the cross. Why is it that we are all so capable of producing a structure which is non-organic and thus defeating our own deepest desires to see the house of God built? How come that we are so capable of this? I will tell you why. Because to produce structures, to produce systems, to reduce things to techniques or methods or regulations is something that we do naturally. It belongs to our natural man. It is us, naturally. To see something organic means that we must know the life of Christ flowing through us, and we cannot know the life of Christ flowing through us unless we know the death of Christ in our experience. Dear child of God, this is our dilemma. The problem is not how to live but how to die. That is the problem that faces us and all the companies that are represented in this room. People continually come and say, "Oh, if we could only know life." My dear friend, that is not the problem. The problem is: "How we can die?" For I will tell you this as sure as I stand here, more surely, if a person dies, God will take care of the resurrection.

Where two or more members of Christ deliberately commit themselves to the death of the Lord Jesus Christ, God will take care of the resurrection.

Now you understand why people say that we are all mystics. It is so much easier to produce a structure, so much easier to produce a system. We only have to get a few Scriptures, and put our heads together, and have a bit of fellowship, so-called, and we can produce some kind of structure, some kind of regulation, some kind of technique, and we can study it everywhere. We can write books on it. We can do all kind of things. But if what I say is true—that the pattern is in the life of Christ and the gifts are in the life of Christ and the functions are in the life of Christ, if the church itself is within the life of Christ, if the very meaning of true fellowship is in the life of Christ in more than one believer, then the great need is to know resurrection life. However, you cannot have resurrection life without death, and you cannot die but by the Spirit.

If you think you can die, try. People are always coming to me and saying, "Oh, I must die; I need to die." You just try. People say, "Could you tell me a book on how to die?" It will only make you heavier than ever. I can give you one or two books that will tell you about the need of dying, but how to die? "Unless a grain of wheat fall into the ground and die, it abideth by itself alone, but if it die, it brings forth much fruit" (John 12:24). The wind is the only thing that makes the grain fall into the ground. The Spirit of God is the only one, once you have seen the need to die, who can bring you to the place where you fall into the ground and die. Maybe He will use your brothers and sisters, maybe He will use your circumstances, maybe He will use your job, maybe He will use some unsaved relative. Maybe, maybe, maybe, but He will take something like the wind of God to come and shake you. You are ready because you have seen the need, and you will fall into the ground and die, by the Spirit.

How did the Lord Jesus die? By the eternal Spirit, He offered Himself up to God without spot or blemish. If our Lord Jesus could not die on the cross apart from the ministry of the Holy Spirit, how much more you? How can you know the death of Christ except by the Holy Spirit? All it becomes is a miserable heaviness; people go around looking dark. As they say in Norway, it is easier to wear black stockings than to have a pure heart.

The fact of the matter is that you can preach the cross and preach the cross and preach the cross until in the end it becomes an obsession. Everyone is heavy and everyone is trying to die, but no one can die because in the end it is the Spirit of God alone who can enable people to die. No one can die of themselves. You must will to do the will of God, but you cannot die.

Oh, how many times I have gotten stuck on that wonderful hymn: "Oh Cross, that liftest up my head, I dare not ask to fly from Thee." I can say that from the fullness of my heart, but then "I lay in dust life's glory dead, and from the ground there blossoms red, life that shall endless be." That is where I get stuck, don't you? There are times when you know you should die. There are times when you know you should lay down your life. There are times when you know you should lose your life. There are times when you know you should deny yourself, but you can't. Your very knowledge that you should do it, only makes you the more miserable. Oh, we poor Christians.

But when the Spirit of God comes and blows upon us, and we are ready, then we do what we cannot naturally do.

Oh, what does it mean, "That I may know Him and the power of His resurrection and the fellowship of His suffering, being made conformable to His death"? (Phillipians 3:10). What does it mean, "being made conformable to His death"? Conformed to His death. No wonder we see so little of church life! No wonder we see so little of the body of Christ in expression! No wonder we experience so little of real fellowship! The problem is that the whole thing is locked up in the life of Christ, but to get the life of Christ really flowing means the death of the cross. Understand me clearly on this matter. We receive life through the death of our Lord Jesus Christ, but to experience life flowing through us we must know what it is to be crucified with Christ. It is by the Spirit that we put to death the deeds of the body. Oh, the problem is not how to live; it is how to die. I have no doubt that there are a thousand situations represented in this place, and every one of them would be solved by dying, some measure of dying.

The Church on Earth

The fact of the matter is that if you and I are going to know church life, if we are going to know fellowship, then two or more brothers or sisters must die by the Spirit. Now, I want to say something here since I am talking about fellowship and not just talking about personal life or personal growth or character. I hope this will lift everything out of the realm of problem for some of you. God does not even require all to die, but a nucleus must die for the rest.

We get into this track where we say, "Do you mean everyone has got to die, everyone has got to die? They will never do it." No, they never will.

Anyone who is looking for the perfect church will never find it. It was Moody who said, "When you join it, it will be imperfect." But we have all got this problem where we are all looking for the perfect church. God never meant the church to be perfect down here! The very evidence that it is the church is that it is imperfect, but it is being perfected.

How can you have a perfect church down here? If all the believers were to gather together in any given locality we would have all kinds of problems. We would have the ones who are lame, the ones who are paralyzed, the ones who are rebellious, the awkward squad of whom God has saved many, and all kinds of states and conditions. We would have young ones and old ones. What is needed? It is not that everyone should die; although of course, it would be wonderful if it would be so. Listen to this, my dear responsible brethren: what God desires is that if you want to see real fellowship in the area in which you live, and you want to see the house of God built up, and you want to see the body of the Lord Jesus Christ expressed, if you want to see something which has got balance within it, you responsible ones have got to die. You may have the most difficult people in the world in your company, but it makes no difference. After all, every company has the devil. You may have the most difficult person in the whole world in your company, but if you will only learn how to die God will use the difficult people to do something in your company.

The Principle of Travail

I would like to say something about travail. The fact of the matter is that if you and I want to see the organic really come, it has to be born. If it is to be born, there must be those who travail. Now we come to God's dilemma—if we can so speak of God having a dilemma—babes cannot travail nor can children. There must be a certain maturity, a certain capacity. The apostle Paul said in Galatians 4:19: "My little children of whom I am again in travail that Christ may be fully formed in you." Again in travail. He travailed over them first when they came to Christ, when they were born of God. This was no cheap evangelism. Here was someone who travailed over these people so that into that place there might come the testimony of Jesus. Here was evangelism with a marvellous panoramic view of the purpose of God. He said, "My little children of whom I am again in travail ..."

Do you know what the problem is? We are all babies. Where can God find those who will travail? The whole company cannot travail. God has to find those who are old enough with enough spiritual capacity, who have not only laid down their lives but this is something further than laying down your life. To lay down your life is one thing; a step further is to be ready for travail. Wouldn't it be an easy thing if those responsible brothers amongst us only had to lay down their lives once and the church would be produced? Oh, how wonderful it would be if we could get it all over with in a few months. But I want to tell you something, dear responsible ones, you are going to have to lay down your lives once and for all, and you will have to lay them down not one time but again and again and again and again and again so that the church of God may be built up, so that the church of God may increase with the increase of God, so that the life of God may flow through, so that the organic may really be known in your midst.

Then dear, dear people of God, there are some of you who are a little older in the Lord and God is preparing you for a ministry of travail. May God help us in these days that lie ahead. We do not have so much time. This is the dilemma of God to find enough spiritual capacity and vision in which the Holy Spirit can conceive something.

The Danger

I want to finish and in some ways I am afraid of ending on a rather negative note. But I want to speak of the terrible danger of contravening this principle. It is much easier to produce a system or a structure or go by regulation or a technique than to walk by the Spirit and to be led by the Spirit. What a judgment this is! It is so much easier to produce something that is Biblical, scriptural but not out of the life of God, than to really walk by the Spirit.

I believe in healing, but I know people who have got some regulation on healing. Oh, it is much easier to have a regulation on healing. A regulation means that everyone should be healed— full stop! Oh, it is much easier to have a regulation; then you have no problem. Well, you have no problems for a while, but then you do get a problem. You get very real problems. Then you have to explain them away and say, "Well, of course, the person was in sin or the person had no faith." Or you have other extraordinary doctrines such as delayed healing, which means that when the person dies, they are healed. Now I find that the most incredible thing I have ever heard. I had a doctor tell me about delayed healing. I said, "What do you mean?" He said, "When they died, they were healed." Then I said, "Do you mean some people are going to heaven with sicknesses and that others get healed?" All of us are healed when we die, thank God. It is much easier to go by a regulation on healing than to go by the Spirit.

What does it mean the prayer of faith will save the sick? It means that the prayer of faith has to be given, but when the prayer of faith is given, God always acts. When it really is the prayer of faith, then God always acts, but it has come out of heaven by the Spirit into us.

The history of the church is full of tragedies—things that apparently began in life and ended in death—doctrines, and systems, and techniques, and methods all brought in, seemingly Biblical, to try and meet some weakness or some dearth or some spiritual impoverishment. At the time as things were growing in number, and everything seemed to be going ahead, it all seemed so wonderful, but it was the undoing of that movement of the Spirit of God. The structure took over and killed it. When this principle is contravened, there is weakness, there is paralysis, there is deception and death.

What do I mean by deception? I mean this. When we contravene this principle and we start to make elders or apostles or whatever we do, we are calling people names that God knows nothing about. It is a deception! A man has been called an apostle and God has never made him an apostle. A man has been called an elder and heaven has never made him an elder. A man has been set aside as a deacon and he is not a deacon. Something is called something else that it is not. It's a deception. Instead of seeking the Lord, inquiring of the Lord, waiting on the Lord for a new release of divine life, we produce our own answer to the need. May God help us!

We need the Lord, and we need Him greatly. I have sought to speak about this principle of the organic, no easy principle to talk about. People normally charge us with mysticism when we talk in terms like this. My dear friends, it is not mysticism; this is spiritual practicality. What is the point of having a system, a structure, a technique, a set of methods, a book of regulations when the sin itself becomes the death of the work of God? Is that being practical? Is that common sense? Never! Spiritual common sense is to recognise that we need the life of God and we need more of the life of God. We need the life of God in abundance. We need an overflow of the life of God. And the only way we can have it is to know what it is to lay down our lives for the Lord and for the brethren. The Spirit of God alone is able to empower us to do that. If for no other reason, every one of us should seek a new release of the Holy Spirit upon us.

Shall we pray?

Now Lord, we do commit this full time into Thy hand. Oh, preserve it, Lord, from misunderstanding or misinterpretation, or those constructions being put upon what has been said which are wrong or imbalanced. Dear Lord, we ask Thee by Thy Holy Spirit to convict us. Oh God, convict us as believers, convict us of the need in our lives to know the death of the cross so that we may know also what it is to walk in newness of life. Oh God, convict us of the need to let go of our lives, to lose our lives for Thy sake and the gospel's that we might find it. Convict us, Lord, of the need that we must fall into the ground and die so that there might be much fruit. Oh Father, preserve us from talking about the church, preaching about the church, dreaming about the church and never experiencing the church. Lord, work, for we ask it in the name of our Lord Jesus Christ. Amen.

6.
Principles of Fellowship–the Supply

Ephesians 4:11–16

And he (our Lord Jesus) gave some to be apostles; and some, prophets; and some, evangelists; and some, pastors and teachers; for the perfecting of the saints, unto the work of ministering, unto the building up of the body of Christ: till we all attain unto the unity of the faith, and of the knowledge of the Son of God, unto a fullgrown man, unto the measure of the stature of the fullness of Christ: that we may be no longer children, tossed to and fro and carried about with every wind of doctrine, by the sleight of men, in craftiness, after the wiles of error; but speaking truth in love, may grow up in all things into him, who is the head, even Christ; from whom all the body fitly framed and knit together through that which every joint supplieth, according to the working in due measure of each several part, maketh the increase of the body unto the building up of itself in love.

Shall we pray?

Dear Lord, we want to bow here in Thy presence and we want to thank Thee that Thou hast made a provision for us. We thank Thee for that provision for cleansing; we thank Thee, Father, for that provision for understanding; we thank Thee for that provision of anointing both for speaking and for hearing. Lord, together now we stand into it. We want to recognize again that apart from Thee we can do nothing. We can neither speak Thy words nor can we hear Thy words apart from Thee, but Lord, Thou hast given us the Holy Spirit that we may know those things which Thou hast given to us. Oh, Lord, we pray together, take this time now and make it live with Thy speaking and with Thy working. Take Thy Word and make it a living reality to our hearts. Maybe Lord, we understand some of these things; give us a clearer understanding. Where it is only an academic understanding, get it into our hearts by Thy Spirit and oh Lord, we pray that Thou will stand against any kind of just mental appreciation of these things. By Thy Spirit, Lord, get it all into us. For we ask it in the name of our Lord Jesus Christ. Amen.

Every Joint Supplies

I would like to speak about another principle of fellowship, the principle of supply. We find that in Ephesians 4:16: "From whom (the Head, even Christ) all the body fitly framed and knit together through that which every joint supplieth." Through that which every joint supplieth, not through that which some of the joints supply, not that through which the most spiritual joints supply, not even through that which most of the joints supply.

It is through that which *every* joint supplies. "Every joint supplies" is the principle of supply.

Colossians 2:19 says: "And not holding fast the Head, from whom all the body, being supplied and knit together through the joints and bands, increaseth with the increase of God." All the body, "being supplied through the joints and bands increaseth with the increase of God."

In Ephesians 4:16 notice another phrase, and in the old version it is a bit of a mouthful. "According to the working in due measure of each several part." In the New American Standard, which I think is one of the best modern translations that we have, it is rendered like this: "According to the proper working of each individual part through that which every joint supplies." It is "every joint, each individual part."

You are constituted by the Lord, through new birth, an individual part of the whole. You are original. You are to be yourself, and yet all that is individualistic is to be dealt with. You are a part of the whole. You do not have every single thing that you can have in yourself. You are a part of a whole—every joint, each individual part—the principle of supply. Every joint supplies something; each individual part properly working.

The trouble with the body of our Lord Jesus Christ down here on earth is that there are an awful lot of disjoints. Anyone would think that the body of our Lord has a case of chronic arthritis. Somehow or other the joints have become stiff and large parts of the body are not properly working. We can talk about all these principles of fellowship—the principle of oneness, of unity, the principle of continuity, the principle of authority, the principle of the organic, but in the end, unless it comes down to this fact that every individual part is properly working, the whole is going to be paralysed. It must be, in one sense, an academic venture, an idealistic venture because in the ultimate it is not only that we must maintain our oneness. It is not only that we need to see that we are part of something which God has been doing through the whole age. It is not only that we must hold fast the Head and really know the Lordship and Headship of Jesus Christ in our midst, but if we are really going to know the organic, every joint has got to supply something and each individual part has got to properly work. Now that means you and me.

The Necessity of Being Built Together

The first thing I would like to say as we look at this matter is to go a little behind it. I want to speak about the necessity of being built together. We are talking about fellowship. Why should we be built with others? Isn't it enough to be saved? Isn't it enough to be redeemed? Why should we be built with others? If some of us feel a little weak and a little in need there may be a point for being built, but surely if we are strong in the Lord, we find everything in our Lord, and we find all that we need in Him, is there really any need to be built with others? Why should we go through all this being knocked about, all this discipline and limitation of having to be bound up with other believers, some of whom are so awkward, and so difficult? Of course, it is always the others that are awkward and difficult; you have probably found that out. If they were all like me it would be such a blissful sort of thing. That is how most of us think. Why should I be built up with others? Why should I contribute to the building? Why is it necessary for me to contribute to the building up of the body, to the building work of God? Why is it important for me to function? Why is it important that I should take responsibility? Can't I go on with the Lord and get to know the Lord personally, get to know His Word deeply in a personal way, grow in the grace and knowledge of Him, and really see the image of the Lord Jesus in myself being worked up and being conformed to His image?

> *Being built upon the foundation of the apostles and prophets, Christ Jesus himself being the chief corner stone; in whom the whole building, fitly framed together, groweth into a holy temple in the Lord; in whom ye also are builded together for a habitation of God in the Spirit." Ephesians 2:20–22*

In whom ye also are builded together for a habitation of God in the Spirit.

> *Unto whom (our Lord Jesus) coming, a living stone, rejected indeed of men, but with God elect, precious, ye also, as living stones, are built up a spiritual house. 1 Peter 2:4*

Mark this: "Ye also, as living stones, are built up a spiritual house, to be a holy priesthood, to offer up spiritual sacrifices, acceptable to God through Jesus Christ." Ye also are built up a spiritual house. He is the living stone; you also are living stones. Together we are built up a spiritual house.

> *In whom each several building, fitly framed together, groweth into a holy temple in the Lord. Ephesians 2:21*

From whom all the body fitly framed and knit together through that which every joint supplies. Ephesians 4:16

Holding fast the Head, from whom all the body, being supplied and knit together. Colossians 2:19

What do all these terms mean: "Groweth up into a holy temple in the Lord ... fitly framed together in Christ ... in whom also you are builded together for a habitation of God in the Spirit ... from whom the whole body fitly framed and knit together ... being supplied and knit together"?

Living Stones Used to Produce the House

One stone does not make a house. A group of stones do not make a house. Many stones do not make a house. All the stones necessary for the building of the house do not make a house. It is the relationship of stone to stone that finally produces a house. If you have a great group of stones and every single one of them is vital for that house, but they have never been related together, never been built together, there has never been anything fitly framed together, you do not have a house. You have all the material, but you do not have a house. It is the relationship of stone to stone which finally produces the house.

Why do you and I need to be built up together with other believers? Why should we contribute to the building work of Christ? Because all this is related to what God has desired from before times eternal. In other words, what God has always desired is a dwelling place in which He can express Himself and reveal

Himself and manifest Himself, as it were, a place in which He can find His home. However we put it—temple, house, bride, body, vine—it comes down to the same thing in the end. It is somehow or other a people who have been brought into a relationship with God through the Lord Jesus Christ and then are built together in the Lord Jesus Christ.

The Bible ends with a marriage, and we discover that that city, which is the wife of the Lamb, that bride of Christ is not just personal. Far from it. We find that it is the relationship of saint to saint in Christ. We find that it is the way they have been brought together, shaped together, built together, fitly framed together, knit together, growing up into Christ as Head—together.

We can talk until we are blue in the face about the bride of Christ, about the city of our God, about the spiritual Zion, about the wife of the Lamb, but unless you and I find our relationship to one another in Christ, in time, and in place, we shall never know the building work of God.

Sometimes people come to me and say, "Ah, what about those poor saints who have seen something and have no fellowship?" They are the exceptions. I always say to those people, "Do you have any fellowship?" They always say, "Yes." We are so deceitful! It is like people who have not come to the Lord, but who come up to you after a gospel message and say, "What about those who have never heard?" Leave that to God! You leave that to God! God is infinitely more just and righteous than you. If you have any sense of justice at all in your heart and mind and conscience it is because God has put it there. It is the palest reflection of the righteousness and justice of God.

Coming back to this matter: leave those poor saints who are out in the wilds somewhere up in Alaska or somewhere else. Are there not believers where *you* live? Are there not some believers who begin to see even dimly some of these things we are talking about? Then, dear child of God, you are caught and you cannot get away. If you want to be part of the bride you have got to allow God to get you into a right relationship with other believers in time and in place. I can talk about being one with all the saints of God behind the Bamboo Curtain or behind the Iron Curtain very conveniently because they are behind the Bamboo Curtain or behind the Iron Curtain. I can even talk about how wonderful it is to be one with saints, and how the Lord is building us together because I hear news from the other side of the world. But God says all that is a lot of hogwash.

The real thing comes down to this: what about the saints in the place where you live? Are you finding your relationship to them and are they finding their relationship to you? Isn't that where we have all our problems? Oh, when we first meet each other we all look such lovely, shining, scrubbed clean saints. However, it is not long before we begin to find that there are a lot of very ugly corners; many, many problems and difficulties that we find with one another. But we have got to find our relationship to one another in the Lord. Otherwise we make a mockery of the Word of God.

I cannot understand this idea, which is such a comfortable idea that has been prevalent for so long in evangelical circles, that being fitly framed together somehow or other all takes place up there in a kind of never, never land. All our being knit together is all in the invisible. It has seemingly no relationship to what is happening down here. If God says that we as living stones have been brought to *the* living stone and are built up as a house, He must mean precisely that. If He says that the whole building, fitly framed together groweth into a holy temple in the Lord, He must mean something.

Finding Our Relationship in the Lord

What does it mean? Does it not mean that we saints have got to find our relationship to one another in the Lord, first to the Head and then to one another in the Lord? It is there in the people of God in time, on this earth, in the locality that I must be trained by the Spirit of God. It is there that I must be changed into the image of Christ. It is there that I must know and submit to discipline. It is there that I must learn obedience by the things which I suffer. It is there that I must exercise responsibility through the grace which God gives to me. It is there that I must fulfil whatever ministry, however small and seemingly insignificant or however great and seemingly significant, it may be. It is there that I must maintain the oneness at all costs, and it is there and there alone that by the grace of God I overcome.

The overcomer is not some kind of legend, some kind of lovely idea that you can get away from all other saints because you and you alone have understood something. You shut yourself away and become like some monk or nun, some hermit of old, and so you overcome. God forbid! The way you overcome is to be in relationship with other saints, and you may have to spend nights in prayer that no one will know about. You may have to suffer in your own heart deeply knowing an anguish and a travail in your heart, but your face is bright so that no one sees that you are spiritually fasting, as it were, unto the Lord. There, in your relationship to other saints in the midst of all the problems, in the midst of all the difficulties, in the midst of all the limitations, in the midst of very, very earthly and human circumstances there and there alone you overcome by the grace of God. In the midst so often of failure and defeat and great downs and so much that is not right, as you overcome, God relates you to those other saints, even the most awkward of them. You discover that it is not to the super and the elite that you get related alone but to all who are in the family of God, and even if they will not have it, you at least have a right relationship toward them. The character of true service must be produced there in time and in place.

The most wonderful thing about being a child of God and about all this building work of God is that we have an eternal vocation in view. All this that God is doing in time and in place is really but a kindergarten; it is a training course. Not that we should devalue what God is doing here, but it is only a training course.

This idea that somehow or other every child of God who is born of the Spirit is willy-nilly granted to sit on a golden throne gracing the mansions of heaven. Oh, may the Lord preserve us! Our Lord never said anything like that. He said, "If we suffer with Him, we shall also be glorified with Him" (see II Timothy 2:12). He said, "To him that overcomes will I grant to sit down in My throne with Me, as I also have overcome and sat down with My Father in His throne" (see Revelation 3:21). The fact of the matter is that the government and administration of God throughout eternity would be in a mess if it were left to most of us Christians in the state that we are in.

God's Work in our Relationship to One Another

Where does God do something in our lives? It is in our relationship to one another. There we learn some of the deepest lessons about God's character. Do we not? We can talk about the love of God and it not mean anything really except that we, in a certain self-centred way, feel that we have been saved and we have been loved. But then we come against someone who is so difficult, so rebellious, so awkward, who is always throwing a spanner in the works[1]. And we say, "Out with him, out with him! We can't put up with this brother anymore. Out with him. He is the problem." God says, "Oh, no, no, no. You have it all wrong. He is not a problem. I could blow on him and he would be finished. You are the problem. You are the problem because of your reaction and your relationship."

Then suddenly we say, "No, Lord. You have it all wrong. I am one of the going-on saints. I am one of those who has understood. So and so does not even see. He is worldly, commercial, fleshly spirit." Then the Lord says, "But I died for him, and I saved him, and I love him." Then we understand something about the love of God we never saw before.

You see, we can go on and on about the love of God, but until we come up against one another in this way, only then can we discover the nature of love and the capacity of love, the infinity

---

1   An expression like the US expression, "throw a wrench in the works," meaning it disrupts a plan, keeping it from succeeding.

of love. We do not really understand love. Then we begin to understand why. Of course, I would not be here if God had not loved me. I am just as difficult, I suppose, in other ways to other people.

I often wonder what it must be like in heaven when all the various prayers and sighs are coming in, thousands and thousands every single second. Someone is saying about so and so: "Oh Lord, do get rid of so and so. They are a problem to this whole place." Then comes another prayer from so and so, "I find so and so really difficult, Lord."

We do have to find our right relationship with one another if anything is going to be done. Stones must be shaped. Stones must be cut. Stones must be polished. Stones must be fitted together. All this work is done where we live now and in our relationships to one another in Christ. Why should I be built together with others? I must be built together with others if I want to be in the city of God. If I want to overcome and sit down with Christ in His throne, if I want to possess the inheritance, which my Lord has given His whole life for, then I must be built with others. Why should I contribute to the building? Because there is no other way for *me* to be built in until *I* start to contribute the little I have.

Each Individual Part Working Properly

Have you ever discovered that the moment you start to give, at that moment you start to discover how poor you are? We can live in a kind of spiritual Fool's Paradise sitting there listening to various ones contributing, meeting, helping, sharing from the Word, loving the saints, (didn't think much of that). We do not know our own need until suddenly we have to take responsibility for someone else. Suddenly, someone comes to the Lord through us. For the first time we have been used by the Lord to lead someone to Christ, and then suddenly we become concerned. We try to help them and we find that we haven't got it in us. We help them in this and that; then we nearly smother them and then we nearly suffocate them. Then the one we led to the Lord gets angry with us. That often happens after a while. He says to us, "I think you are stuffy." We suddenly find when we begin to take responsibility that there is real need in our own lives and that, in turn, if we mean business, will drive us on to the Lord.

What I am trying to say is that each individual part has got to work properly. Every single part. All increase, all development is according to the proper working of each individual part. You know what it is when some small muscle, almost unrecognised muscle up to that point as far as you are concerned, gets a cold in it and seizes up. Oh, what pain! Or one joint gets inflamed—oh, the pain that one joint can give! Sometimes it is just a small area that gets infected, but the whole body feels it.

I wonder sometimes in those companies represented here whether you are one of those painful spots because you have seized up. You have got a cold, a spiritual cold. Maybe someone dealt with you harshly. Maybe you felt that somehow or other someone said something about you that was unkind. Maybe you have been misrepresented, and you have got a cold. Your love has just gone cold and you say, "What's the use? They are like that! So what's the use?" You have got a cold. You are not only damaging the body, you are damaging yourself. Or maybe you have been a joint of supply. You have given something and then got inflamed. Some infection set in, and you just got inflamed. There are all kinds of infections that can get in—devices of the enemy, imbalance, something else. The joint gets inflamed and then something happens to the whole body. Not only is the body damaged, but you are also.

What is this principle of supply? I think everyone of us here probably sees the need that we should all work together, that every individual part should be properly working, that every joint should be supplying something. What is this principle of supply? It is found in Matthew 10:8: "... freely ye received, freely give." Give what you have received; that is the principle of supply. You have received something; give it. Do not give what you have not received. That is where we get so much problem.

People are always contributing what they have not received. There is someone who has a gift of singing, and just because they have a gift of singing everyone says, "Sing. Sing. Please sing." It is not that the gift, their talent for singing has gone through the cross and been broken by the Lord and filled with the Spirit. Oh, don't let us be silly about this. Sometimes someone's singing can bring the Lord to us. Don't be afraid of it as if to say, "Oh, that is all the world; that is entertainment." Sometimes someone can have a gift like that which has gone right through the cross and there is something in it of a quality that was never there before. One person can play the piano and it is a natural gift, but all you get is them. Another person can play the piano and all you receive is the Lord. What is the difference? They may both have musical degrees. What is the difference? One person can be a whiz on the piano and yet all you get left with is them. Oh, the way their fingers run over the keys. Oh, it is so beautiful, but all you get is them. Another person can play and you receive the Lord. Why? Because that natural gift has gone into a melting pot and has been broken by the Lord. Then it has been given back in resurrection and filled with the Spirit. Then it becomes a channel of grace. It becomes a joint of supply.

I have only used two extreme things, singing and music, but it goes into everything. We often think: "Here is a person who can organize. He is a great organizer. He is a gift to the church." We get him right away. Oh, how America has suffered! Haven't you felt it? I have never seen a more organized place in the whole of my life. You go into some churches and they are so organized that really you almost feel your breathing has been organized for you. Every single thing is programmed. The children are programmed, the young people are programmed, the older people are programmed, the money is programmed, the meetings are programmed. Everything is programmed, programmed, programmed. We need organising ability when it has gone into the breaking of the Lord Jesus, and when it has come out into resurrection and been filled with the Spirit. What a gift it is!

Here is someone with a gift, as we say in Ireland, "the gift of the gab." That is, they just have a natural gift for talking. They could talk, as we say again in Ireland, "the hind legs off a donkey." For them to talk is the most natural thing in the whole wide world. They can talk and talk and talk, and if once they get saved they talk; only this time they talk Biblical talk. So we say, "Ah, so and so is a preacher." We immediately get them into theological seminary, and through theological seminary into church, and dress them up, ordain them, and now we have got the minister. From then on he goes on with the gift of the gab. It is no problem for him to speak because it is easy for him; it is natural to him. That is the problem. But oh, isn't it wonderful when God can take such a gift of communication, a natural gift, and put it into the breaking, as it were, of the cross, and through into resurrection, and then fill it with the Spirit and anoint it with the Spirit. Then there can be something wonderful under the government and control of the Lord.

The principle of supply. Don't give what you have got naturally. Give what you have received from the Lord. Jesus said these words: "Heal the sick, raise the dead, cleanse the lepers, cast out demons; freely ye received, freely give." And these dear ones went out, and here is an amazing thing. They did not even know the Lord deeply. They had no experience of the cross or the Spirit, yet they went out and they saw the most incredible things happen. They saw the lepers cleansed. They saw demons cast out. They saw the sick healed, and they saw Satan, as Jesus said, "falling as lightning from heaven." Why? Because they simply obeyed this one law of supply—give what you have received. Don't give what you have naturally but give what you have received. If our Lord has given you something, give it. If you are born of God, you have something of the Lord, haven't you? Give what you have of the Lord. This is the principle of supply. Don't overreach yourself.

Don't Overreach Yourself

Let me speak to those who are younger in the Lord. When you come into a time like this and you hear all these wonderful people talking about things like the overcomer, and spiritual warfare, and the nature of the church and being built together, "Oh!" You think, "I have never heard such things in my life." Then you try to overreach yourself. When it comes to a time of praise you either say, "It's no good; it's no good. I can't open my mouth and praise the Lord. Why, with all those wonderful brothers there and those tremendous sisters, it would be stupid." The Lord would say "Who does so and so think they are praising Me this morning with all these wonderful people here in the front row?"

Do you know there are times when a baby's cry means more to Father than anything else? You see, if the baby tries to be a university graduate that would be stupid. Father would say, "There is something wrong with this child." But so many of God's children are trying to be university graduates spiritually before their time. They try to take on the language and overreach and say, "Oh-h Lo-o-ord," and they start talking about things they do not know the first thing about. And then the whole thing becomes artificial, and God says, "Oh, dear, dear, I do not get any joy out of this." You have overreached yourself. You started by giving what you had received and then you went on to what you have not received. The principle of supply is to give what you have received.

Dear young child of God, have you found the Lord? Why don't you open your mouth next time we have a time of open praise and say, "Thank You, Lord, for saving me." That means more to the Lord than if you say, "Oh Lord, I thank You for the book of Revelation and how the overcomers have gotten through in those seven churches, Lord, and then those standing on Mount Zion with the Lamb, following Him withersoever He goes." The Lord says, "Look here, you haven't seen that. What do you mean talking to Me like this? Why don't you just praise Me for what I am?"

Give What You Have Received

Do you know there are times when we have people take part in prayer and they give us a whole potted version of the Sermon on the Mount? I feel sometimes the Lord says, "Oh dear, dear, dear. I gave that. Why does he have to give it all back to Me? Why can't he simply say, 'Lord, I adore You.'" But somehow or other some of us cannot do that, cannot actually say with our lips, "I love You, Lord," in front of all these people. We just cringe, but we can give a paraphrase of some book. It is not real. Better to tell the Lord that you love Him with all your heart and be real. Then there comes out to God a warmth and there comes back from God a warmth to you, and the whole body is warmed. Oh, if we could be joints of supply! If we would only give what we each have to give! Some of you are suffering from a kind of introversion. When you hear wonderful things, you say, "I can't do that." Don't worry about that; you will. The only way you will get to where those others have gotten is by being yourself in Christ. As you give what you have received from the Lord, so shall you get more. It is the principle of supply.

> *Give, and it shall be given unto you; good measure, pressed down, shaken together, running over, shall they give into your bosom. For with what measure ye mete it shall be measured to you again. Luke 6:38*

What a wonderful word! Give and it shall be given unto you. How? "Good measure, pressed down, shaken together, running over, shall they give into your bosom. For with what measure ye mete it shall be measured to you again." Do you want to know what the principle of supply is? Give the little you have of the Lord. Share it. That is fellowship. Share the little you have of the Lord. Don't go beyond. However little it is, share it. If you have just been saved, share that. If your testimony is of salvation, share that. If it goes further, share more. But give what you have received and it shall be given unto you, and as you give you get more back. Give then what you get back, and you will get even more. Oh, here is the way to be spiritually avaricious. Give what you receive of the Lord and you will get more. Give the more you receive and you will get even more. Give the even more and you will get even more than that.

You see, some people sit down and say, "Until the Lord comes to me with a spiritual blockbuster and sort of blows me one thousand miles ahead in the path to the kingdom I am not going to contribute a single thing." My dear friend, you never will. You will go to the Lord without having grown hardly at all except in your head. You will not get anywhere. The only way to get anywhere spiritually is to be a joint of supply. What you receive from the Head, pass on and share. Don't overreach yourself but share. For it is a principle with the Lord that whatever a man gives he gets back.

I have never failed to be amazed by the Dead Sea, finding all its sources in the snows of the Hermon range. It begins as three or four little sources and always, even at the height of the dry hot season those waters are always sparkling and cool for they come from all the melted snow which goes deep down into great walls, as it were, inside Mount Hermon. Wherever that water comes into the Jordan River it brings life even where they have piped it all the way through the Plain of Sharon down to the Negev. Wherever it comes, it brings life. You can see an arid wilderness on both sides of the River Jordan but where the river goes it is all fertile. Yet the whole of that river, with all its millions of gallons of water per day, flowing into the Dead Sea and still not a thing lives in the Dead Sea—not a shrimp, not a crab, not a fish, nothing, not even a bit of seaweed. Nothing lives in the Dead Sea. How is it that it can take all that life-giving water and turn it into sterility? Simple. The Dead Sea takes everything and gives nothing. The Dead Sea has no outlet. It takes every single thing it can and gives absolutely nothing. Therefore, it is the Dead Sea.

There are believers, there are companies that will take every single thing the Lord has for them and turn the whole thing into sterility. It becomes sterile. They can revel in the doctrines of the resurrection of Christ, in the ascension of Christ, in the fullness and anointing of the Holy Spirit, and in many other matters, but somehow every single thing that comes to them they make sterile. No one ever gets saved. There is never any new movement of the Lord because there is no outlet. The principle of supply is that you have got to give what you have received. It is true individually; it is true corporately. Fellowship is just the sharing of our Lord Jesus Christ. "God is faithful through whom you were called into the fellowship of His Son Jesus Christ our Lord," (1 Corinthians 1:9). We are sharing what we have of the Lord.

Being a Joint of Supply in Open Times

May I say some practical things about this matter? I have sought to explain a little bit of this principle of supply, whether it is in the corporate and wider level, or whether it is your individual part in the whole. The fact is that we have to give what we have received, and when we give what we have received, we receive more.

What is the practical need? I believe first of all we need in the life of the church of God in any given place, not only times of teaching and times of the ministry of the Word, but times when the whole of our time is open to the Spirit of God for the exercise of the priesthood of all believers. We brethren need to see this. We need to see that in the life of the people of God we need to have times, which are entirely open to the Spirit of God to lead so that we may learn to follow the Spirit of God, learn to discern the anointing in a gathering, how to distinguish the anointing, how to abide under the anointing, how to keep under the anointing, and therefore keep in life, right the way through the meeting. We learn tremendous lessons this way.

Then, may I say something else about being a joint of supply? All those of us who do not have any responsibility of leadership need to be open to the Lord. We do not just give anything we have got, just like that because we happen to have it. There must be a time. Some people come to a meeting and say, "I have a hymn; I am going to give it anyway because I have this hymn *burning* in me." So the first available opportunity they just say it. That is not the proper working of each individual part. My body doesn't just work sort of all independently.

In our open time the Holy Spirit is sovereign, and if you have something, there will come a correct time and you will know it by the Spirit as we move through. There is a time for you to contribute what you have, however little or however much, under the government of the Spirit of God. We do not just give what we have willy-nilly because we happen to have it. Even the timing of its giving must be under the Spirit of God and in relationship with the rest of the members of the body.

Being a Joint of Supply in Leadership

May I say something to you who are more responsible brothers in companies? I believe that to be a joint of supply in this matter means that when you have open times you must get together beforehand and cover those times. One of the great tragedies at present is the way people drift into meetings. They say because the Lord is with us and it is going to be an open time no one takes any responsibility. We just drift together and then we spend the first half hour wandering, and only just before the meeting comes to a close do we get anywhere. Those of you who are responsible brothers, if God has given you responsibility, you have to lay down your life. In this sense it means you have to give even more time than anybody else. Otherwise, you should not have the responsibility. We have to meet beforehand sometimes to govern the time, to proclaim that Jesus is Lord over the time, to use keys to lock up what is not of Himself and to unlock what is of Himself. We must declare that Jesus Christ is Lord. Always recognize the lordship of Jesus Christ.

One of the things the Lord has shown us in Richmond[2] is that the leading brethren have no rights whatsoever. We meet always at least twenty minutes or half an hour before every gathering, and we do not spend the time just talking. We get on our knees and really cover that time before the Lord. Sunday morning we will be together with any of the other brothers who wish to come with us from about 10:15 to 10:50, our time begins at 11:00. On the weeknight we will meet together at 7:10 for the time beginning at 7:30.

I remember a while ago when we came to the conclusion that we brothers had got to get together on a Monday evening, and we said, "We can't do it; we just can't do it. We are all so busy." The brothers who were married said, "How can we do it? Can we give another time?" But we felt that if we didn't, everything was going to suffer. To be a joint of supply means that we have got to get together. So we began on a Monday evening, just we responsible ones getting together and then we opened it to anyone who had complaints, or suggestions, or who needed counsel, or prayer or help. We are there now, every Monday evening from 5:30 to 9:00, and that is another evening gone. But if God has done anything amongst us I believe it is partly due to the fact that there are some brothers who have fallen into the ground and died. That is real headship. That is not just throwing your weight around and saying, "We are the boss. You do what we say. You do this and this and this." It is being pioneers in sacrifice and pioneers in laying down our lives for the brethren. That we must do as a joint of supply.

---

2 At Halford house in Richmond, Surrey

What a wonderful thing it is in our gathering together when this principle of supply is evident! We make a big mistake if we think we are only the church when we are gathered. We are the church at all times, and we are to be joints of supply, with each individual part properly working at all times. Nevertheless, when we come together we can take the temperature of the whole church. In an open time you can quickly see whether this principle of supply is in operation or whether it is being contravened.

Be careful of hiding behind singing. It is a wonderful thing to sing praises to the Lord as it says in Ephesians 5: "Singing one to another in psalms and hymns and spiritual songs" (see v. 19). Be careful that we do not hide behind endless singing as if that alone is praise. Sometimes we need to open our lips and praise the Lord one after another. Sometimes I do not think it is such a bad idea to all praise the Lord together. You can get rid of a lot of inhibition that way. After all the Lord is hearing all those thousands of prayers of the saints at the same time every twenty-four hours and sorts them all out. But it is a lovely thing to lead one another in praise. Sometimes it is a good thing to praise the Lord all together; just praise Him and worship Him with a volume of praise.

We need to be a joint of supply. There are times when we need to have something from the Word—a word of exhortation when someone has had a revelation from the Lord which they can share under the government of God. There is nothing more wonderful than an open time when the Holy Spirit is in charge. How He leads us!

Being a Joint of Supply Outside Our Gatherings

May I say something finally about outside our gatherings? We need to be a joint of supply outside our gatherings, too. There are all kinds of ways we can help one another. Some people have just been saved, but they do not know what to do. There may be a brother who is so busy in the work of God and so weighed down, maybe you can go and do some practical job that would release him. Some of you older brothers can help some of those who are in full responsibility by just doing a practical job that you can do which would certainly lift something from them. It is such a practical way, but some of us can only think of being a joint of supply as far as the platform is concerned. If we are on the platform that is being a joint of supply. If we are anywhere else we are nothing. But God rewards people in the end who do practical things that help others who have big responsibilities. There are some people who pray for us and only God knows it; but they labour in prayer behind the scenes. They will share in any reward that comes from such ministry because they have undertaken a laborious task which has no glamour, no romance, and no popular recognition. But it is being a joint of supply.

Oh, if only we could see this thing! Maybe someone is ill. Now let me get this quite clear. Sometimes the principle is this: everyone should bear his or her own burden. Never do anything that will make another member of the body lazy. But on the other hand, there are times when being a joint of supply is a very practical thing. Here is a sister who is not well. What a wonderful thing it is when some other sisters go and say, "Look, we want to help you. Tell us what we can do so that we can just be of help to you." Isn't that a practical way? Do you know what happens? That dear sister who is way down there, has not been able to praise the Lord, but suddenly because of the joints of supply she praises the Lord.

I was speaking about this in a company a while ago and I happened to say this: I think maybe the best way you can be a joint of supply is by going to somebody and cutting their lawn. An old sister came up to me afterwards. She had been a prayer warrior in that particular company and she said, "Brother, I probably shouldn't tell you this. I have had my whole hip taken out and a new one put in. When I went to surgery, one of the responsible brothers in this company came to me and asked if there was anything he could do. I said to him, "The thing I am worrying about is the garden. I will not be able to do it now for nine months." The brother said to her, "We will cut it," and he charged her. When she came back, she found that it had not been cut. Then she said, "Some dear brother came and cut it and will not take a penny. When you said that about praising the Lord this morning, I thought to myself: I was so down and I tried to get over it all, but every time I looked out of the window all I could see was a forest. I worried and worried about what my neighbours would think. What about my testimony here as a believer? When that young brother came in with his bright face and cut the whole thing, which was really hard work because the one who had taken the money did not do it, I got on my knees and worshipped the Lord." That is a joint of supply!

Dear sisters, bake a cake now and again for somebody. Send a bunch of flowers now and again to somebody. Go and visit somebody. You may be a joint of supply. You see, we tend to think that it is only if we have got some sort of tremendous spiritual message that we will be a joint of supply. However, we can do the most practical things and we become a joint of supply in the body of Christ because we release something precious of the Lord in someone else. What a wonderful thing to be like that!

To those of you sisters who are married, let me just say one thing from 1 Timothy 5:14. Remember, your job is your home. I believe that the home of the married sister is her ministry in the house of God. It says, "Rule the household." I have been in some places where the husbands will not allow their wives to make a single decision regarding their home. I know one brother who will not even allow his wife to dress in the colours she wants to dress in. I remember another occasion where a brother would not even allow his sister to pray when in his presence. He had the idea that she was not permitted to pray at any time when a man was present.

Dear sisters, if you read Proverbs 31 you will have a very big shock about the sister who is above price. This sister goes down and buys a field and produces things on it and she weaves and spins and sews it. What a remarkable thing! It is quite foreign to some of the ideas in some Christian circles. Here is a sister who is in a right relationship to her husband, in subjection to him, but she is ruling her household. She is not letting him have all the worries. She is ruling her household; that is her ministry. When decisions about policy have to be taken, it is the husband, but she is ruling her household. Dear sisters, be a joint of supply. Your homes can be places of hospitality. Your homes can be places of ministry. If nothing else, your children are a God-given heritage. May the

Lord help us to be joints of supply, not only in our gatherings but outside of our gatherings, and in our homes as well.

Shall we pray?

Dear Lord, this finds all of us out—the proper working of each individual part. Oh Lord, Thou knowest how so many of us are not properly working. Lord, by Thy Spirit stir us. Some of us need to know what it is to stir up the gift that is within us. Others of us need to know what it is just to take that step in faith and share the little we have of Thee with our brothers and sisters. Some of us need our eyes opened to that great range of practical things that we can do which make it so much easier for the rest of the saints. Oh Lord, help us. Grant that we may be joints of supply in the body of our Lord Jesus Christ. We ask it in His name. Amen.

7.
Principles of Fellowship–Spiritual Vision

Ephesians 1:15–23

For this cause I also, having heard of the faith in the Lord Jesus which is among you, and the love which ye show toward all the saints, cease not to give thanks for you, making mention of you in my prayers; that the God of our Lord Jesus Christ, the Father of glory, may give unto you a spirit of wisdom and revelation in the knowledge of him; having the eyes of your heart enlightened, that ye may know what is the hope of his calling, what the riches of the glory of his inheritance in the saints, and what the exceeding greatness of his power to us-ward who believe, according to that working of the strength of his might which he wrought in Christ, when he raised him from the dead, and made him to sit at his right hand in the heavenly places, far above all rule, and authority, and power, and dominion, and every name that is named, not only in this world, but also in that which is to come:

---

and he put all thing in subjection under his feet, and gave him to be head over all things in the church, which is his body, the fulness of him that filleth all in all.

Shall we pray?

Oh beloved Lord, we bow before Thee with full hearts. We thank Thee for all that Thou art to us. We thank Thee for Thy salvation. We thank Thee for Thy life. We thank Thee for Thy fullness. We thank Thee for all the resources which ours in Thee. We thank Thee beloved Lord for Thy power and authority and now as we bow before Thee we want to tell Thee that as we come to this last time of these days together we need Thee, and we need Thee to give to us that Spirit of wisdom and revelation in the knowledge of Thyself. Oh Lord, we pray that Thou wilt deliver us from a mere academic understanding of the things that are being said and what Thou has been seeking to do.

Lord, we pray that the eyes of our heart might be enlightened that we might know these things in a direct and original way. Oh Lord, cause Thy light to shine into our hearts and enable us to see light in Thy light. Lord, wilt Thou grant we pray that Thy Word may live to us all and may dwell in our hearts richly in all wisdom and knowledge. Lord, we thank Thee that the anointing is ours in the Lord Jesus Christ, and by faith now we come to stand into it, speaker and hearer alike. We open our spirits to Thyself that thou wilt fill us afresh and give and manifest that enabling power not only to speak Thy Word but to hear

Thy Word, and we shall give to Thee all the praise and the glory and the thanksgiving through our Lord Jesus Christ. Amen.

The Necessity of Spiritual Vision

There is one burden in my heart that I would like to share with you, finally. We have said so much about fellowship, but the burden of my heart is that God would give us vision, that He would really open the eyes of our heart and give to us that Spirit of wisdom and revelation in the knowledge of our Lord Jesus Christ. I always get such a fear when I see everything going into notebooks. Conferences are dreadful places because people sit there taking notes. I am not against it being taken down when there is a shining into the hearts and when there is vision. But oh, the danger of just storing knowledge, of just accumulating doctrinal and biblical truth. What we need above every other thing is that the Lord should reveal Himself to us, that with the eyes of our heart we would see the Lord.

I believe that spiritual vision is an absolute necessity, and I venture to say that as we move into the last phase of this age spiritual vision will be the determining factor as to whether we shall go through or break up. Our adherence or loyalty to truth, academically or mentally understood, will not stand us in good stead when the trial of our faith comes in all its severity. It is only what a man or a woman has seen that will have so apprehended them that they will be unable to deny. The apostle Paul said, "Wherefore, O king Agrippa, I was not disobedient to the heavenly vision" (Acts 26:19).

Understanding the Mind of God

Of course, I want to say straight away what I mean when I speak of the necessity of spiritual vision. I am not talking here about *visions*. There may be a place for visions, there may be a place for dreams, but I am not talking about visions. I am talking about vision, understanding the Lord, understanding the will of God, understanding the time in which we live, understanding the purpose of God concerning the Lord Jesus Christ and those who have been brought into Him through His finished work. Perception. Spiritual seeing. Understanding. That is what we need above every other thing.

In Proverbs 29:18 it says, "Where there is no vision the people perish" (KJV). "Where there is no vision the people cast off restraint" (ASV). The Hebrew word for "cast off restraint" comes from the binding up of a woman's hair. It simply means that when you take it out, the whole lot falls down. It is the word we find concerning the children of Israel when they worshipped the golden calf. They had cast off restraint and were dancing and worshipping the golden calf.

This word *vision* in Hebrew is the thought of teaching or prophetic understanding. It is not just the other word in Hebrew for seeing a picture, having a vision in that way, but it is an understanding of the Lord's Word and His way. You will remember in I Samuel it says: "There was no open vision in those days" (see 3:1). In other words, there was no prophetic word, there was no prophetic understanding, no interpretation of the mind of God, no understanding of the mind of God in those days.

Now let me say this straight away. Where there is no understanding of the ways of the Lord, sooner or later the people perish; they go to pieces. It does not matter if they are redeemed of the Lord or not, the principle is the same. Where there is no understanding of the Lord, no understanding of the ways of the Lord, no seeing of the Lord, no understanding of His purpose, then there is no cohesion. There is no direction. There is, as it were, nothing that holds us all together into one and keeps us moving together and flowing together. We perish; we go to pieces.

The Spirit of Wisdom and Knowledge

When writing that great letter to the Ephesians, perhaps the most tremendous revelation, in one sense, in the whole Bible is when the apostle Paul comes to a point at the very beginning where he suddenly stops and says to the person to whom he is dictating the letter, "I wonder if we ought to put in this prayer burden of mine for them all." Then he evidently feels, "I think we should." So he stopped his thought for a moment and said, "For this cause I bow my knees to the God and Father of our Lord Jesus Christ that He may grant to you a spirit of wisdom and revelation in the knowledge of the Lord Jesus, having the eyes of your heart enlightened that you may know what is the hope of His calling and what the riches of the glory in the saints, and what the exceeding greatness of his power to us-ward who believe" (Ephesians 1:15–19). In other words, the apostle Paul was terrified that that letter would just become an academic literary object, that it might become, as it were, just the ground for "Bible studies," that it might become sermon material, or become a means of some people getting a livelihood producing Bible outlines, little sermons, or little messages. "No!" said the apostle Paul. "If once we begin to reduce this, which God has shown me—this heavenly vision, this understanding of God's purpose concerning the Lord Jesus—into human language, once we define it in human words, then they will take it academically. They will think that if they can just get it up here in the head, they have got it." God preserve us from people who have got it up there in their head. They are the biggest menace the church has got. Some of us tend to think that the greatest menace and danger to the work of God are those people who are ignorant of the purpose of God. Yes, in one way, but an even greater menace are those people who have it "up here" but have no understanding of it. They can give us outlines and define truth, but when it comes to the practice of it, they do not know the first thing about it.

The apostle Paul stopped and put the whole lot down and said, "Now listen, everyone who reads this letter, I want you to know that for those to whom primarily it was written, I got on my knees and I prayed, "Oh God, the Father of our Lord Jesus Christ, the Father of glory, don't let this letter be just academic. Don't let it stay in the realm of mental appreciation, just in the realm of doctrinal truth. Lord, give to those who are the recipients of this letter that spirit of wisdom, understanding, and revelation in the knowledge of the Lord Jesus.

The apostle Paul explained his whole experience in Galatians 1:15–16 in these terms: "But when it was the good pleasure of God, who separated me, even from my mother's womb, and called me through his grace, to reveal his Son *in* me." It was not even to reveal His Son *to* me, but to reveal His Son *in* me. It is absolutely true that the apostle had a vision of our Lord on the road to Damascus, but it was much more than just something dramatic and sensational. For when the apostle saw the Lord, he saw something tremendous. He said, "When it pleased God to reveal His son *in* me." From the very beginning of his conversion, in his salvation, he began to understand that he had been incorporated into Christ; he became one with Christ.

This matter of vision is therefore a principle. I cannot say it is a principle of fellowship necessarily, but it is a general principle in the whole work of God. It is a necessity not a luxury. Many of us tend to think that somehow or other such vision is only granted to the elite amongst the people of God, for those who are going to be very greatly used in the Lord's service. However, this is not something for a special inner circle nor is it a luxury, with which you will be greatly blessed if you should have it. It is a necessity, dear child of God, for every single one of us. In the days of shaking and sifting into which we are surely coming, in the days that lie ahead when the enemy will do every single thing possible to withstand the work of God, to destroy the building work of God, and to somehow halt the completion of the building of the house of God, we must be, above everything else, men and women of vision.

Abraham Saw the Glory of God

It does not matter where we turn in the Word of God we find this matter. People seem to think that it was perhaps just something in the New Testament. No, no it isn't. Really everything began with Abraham and it all began with Abraham with vision.

What did Stephen say in Acts 7:2? "The God of glory appeared unto our father Abraham when he was in Ur of the Chaldees in Mesopotamia." *The God of glory appeared unto our father Abraham when he was in Ur of the Chaldees in Mesopotamia.* That is how it all began. There is this idea that is so common in some circles that Abraham was some smelly, illiterate, Bedouin shepherd wandering around the desert with a few straggly goats and sheep and a camel. The idea is that he could neither read nor write and did not have an ounce of education in him. Abraham was nothing of the kind at all!

He came from Ur of the Chaldees, which was one of the great cities of antiquity. It was a city that was a proud, sophisticated civilization. Did you know that a lot of ladies' fashionable jewellery today is modelled on those pieces of jewellery that were found in Ur of the Chaldees? It had its ladies' hairdos coiffures. It had its banks. It had its stock exchange. It had its postal service. Ur of the Chaldees had all kinds of things. Of course, we understand from the Talmud a little more about Abraham. We understand that he was the idol maker. His family controlled the whole business of making idols for the whole city. It was while he was making idols one day that he thought to himself (so the Talmud says) "Isn't it strange that we make these things and then bow down to them?"

Then the Father of glory appeared to him. We do not know how, but Abraham saw the Lord. He did not just see God; he saw the God of glory. Now if we had Abraham here this morning, I could sit down certainly. He was not limited in his understanding. He not only saw the day of the Messiah, he not only saw the gospel from afar, but even more remarkable it says this: "By faith Abraham when he was called went out not knowing whither he went, for he looked for the city which has the foundations, whose builder and maker or architect is God" (see Hebrews 11:8–10). Where did Abraham get any idea of a city? He had to let go of a city. He went out to become a sojourner in the desert. He went out to live in tents. He never ever settled in a city. The only city he ever saw was when he fell away from the Lord and went down into Egypt and said Sarah was his sister and got into a lot of trouble. In actual fact, it says Abraham looked for the city that had *the* foundations.

When the God of glory appeared to Abraham, he suddenly saw that this long enduring, sophisticated, civilized, educated, city of Ur did not have foundations. Maybe if you had been in Ur of the Chaldees in the same way as when you go to Washington today, you would think this would never disappear. These magnificent buildings, these wonderful avenues, these wonderful monuments, this great system of civilization, this capital of a great, great super power will never disappear. It will. If the Lord tarries the whole thing will one day disappear as surely as Ur of the Chaldees has disappeared. It was a tremendous step for Abraham, knowing the whole city of Ur of the Chaldees with its boulevards, avenues, buildings, and monuments, and its sophistication with its whole system of education, to suddenly realise that the city did not have the foundations.

Do you know Abraham saw more than many true believers in the new covenant? How many real believers see what the city of God is? Very few indeed. They just look at you as if you are crazy if you start talking about the city of God. All they know are hymns like, "treading streets of gold," and pearly gates opening, and sort of having cups of tea in some heavenly city. That is all they can understand about the city of God, but it is a Sunday school idea. What Christian has seen what Abraham saw over four thousand years ago? Where did Abraham see the city which has the foundations? He didn't see some plan of a city. He didn't see some physical city. When he saw the God of glory, he saw in the God of glory the city of God. By seeing the Lord he saw the face of God's glory. He saw the dwelling place of God's glory, and from that moment Abraham was spoilt. He was never the same again.

Any man or woman who sees something of the Lord is spoilt for anything else. Once the God of glory appears to us we are never the same again. We have seen something. We are no longer inhabitants of earthly cities. We are sojourners and pilgrims. We have seen the city which has the foundation, whose builder and maker is God. Oh, Abraham saw so much, but the least of those in the body of Christ under the new covenant are greater than these Old Testament saints in their privileges. Do you realise how you are devaluing your status in Christ if you do not even see what the city of God is? Abraham saw it and it changed his whole life. It changed his lifestyle. It changed his whole direction for time and eternity. Have you been gripped by something like that? That is vision. God began everything with Abraham with vision. The God of glory appeared unto our father Abraham.

Jacob Saw the Lord

I would like to talk more about some of the others. I would like to talk about Jacob, for Jacob saw the Lord. That great swindler, that great twister, the biggest twister in the Middle East, when he saw the Lord his name *Jacob* which means "twister" was changed to *Israel* which means "God persists." "Thou art a prince with God," playing on the word, because God persists. Can you be anything else but a Calvinist? Jacob saw the Lord and when he saw the Lord something happened. He was given a change of names, and his name was to be the name of the people of God throughout all time—Israel.

Moses Saw the Lord

I want to go on to Moses. It all began with vision with Moses. He had an academic understanding when he was younger. Moses was the adopted son of Pharaoh's daughter, brought up in a palace. Again, if we understand some of those things that are extra-biblical, if they are truth and not myth, and there is no reason to believe that they are just myths simply because they are extra-biblical, we understand from the Talmud that Moses was the hero of the Libyan campaign and highly decorated by Pharaoh for his victories in that campaign. We only get a hint of this in the Bible where we are told that he esteemed the reproach of Christ far greater than the riches of Egypt and the pleasures of sin (see Hebrews 11). But Moses only academically saw something, and when he saw an Egyptian fighting with a Hebrew he stepped in and slew the Egyptian and then fled for his life. For forty years he was in the backside of the desert keeping a lot of silly sheep. Once the son of Pharaoh's daughter, now he was keeping sheep. Sheep were greatly despised by the Egyptians.

Forty years! I suppose for the first ten years Moses thought of visitations from God and how he was going to be carried back to Egypt on a great flood of revival to his people, but it never happened. Twenty years went by and he got a little more modified, but he still believed that something was going to happen. Thirty years went by and it was beginning to get a little bit difficult, but he held onto the idea that somehow or other something was going to happen. But when the forty years were up, the whole matter had died in him.

Then one day in the desert, keeping his sheep, he saw a fire in the desert. Now those of us who have lived in the desert have seen those fires. I remember the first time I saw one I asked the Bedouin who was with me at the time, "What is that fire out there?" He said, "That is one of those thorn bushes. It is dead and dried up, and it has ignited. The sun has ignited it." Moses never took any notice of it; he just saw a fire in the desert and went on dreaming his dreams. Then he looked back ten minutes later and it was still burning, and he went on dreaming his dreams. In twenty minutes he looked again at it and said, "That really is some bush," and went on dreaming his dreams. In half an hour he looked and said, "That must be the biggest thorn bush in the desert." I suppose either then or maybe at forty minutes he thought, "I will go over and see this great sight." He went over to where this thorn bush was burning and when he got to it, I have no doubt that it was not a very big thorn bush, he saw that the bush burned with fire, but the bush was not consumed. Then out of the thorn bush, out of the flame of fire in the thorn bush, the voice of God came: "Moses, Moses, do not draw nigh; take the shoes from off your feet for the ground whereon you stand is holy ground. I am the God of your fathers, the God of Abraham, Isaac, and Jacob," (see Exodus 3:5–6).

Then He went on to reveal Himself. Moses saw the Lord and he saw Him in a thorn bush. This was to transform the whole life and direction of Moses. For when he saw the Lord in the thorn bush, Moses saw himself. It was as if God was saying, "Dear Moses, you are just like this old dried-up thorn bush—no value, ugly, worthless, insignificant and full of thorns. You are like that Moses. You thought you were a great palm tree once, stately and majestic. I have reduced you to a dried-up thorn bush. You thought you were an acacia tree, the loveliest tree in the desert out of which the tabernacle furniture was made, but I have reduced you to a dried-up, dead old thorn bush. You thought you were a fig tree, full of the Spirit, but I have reduced you to a dried-up old thorn bush, Moses. You are the dried-up old thorn bush, Moses—commonplace, worthless, ugly and prickly, and I am the fire. Moses, when I get into you and you come into Me, then My purpose will be fulfilled."

Moses said, "Who shall I say sent me?" Do you know what God said to Moses out of the thorn bush? God said, "I AM, that is My name. Not I was, not I will be, but I AM that I AM. Go and tell them I AM in the midst of the thorn bush has spoken to you." It was as if God gave Moses a blank cheque.

People often get frightened of that name I AM that I AM, and they think that it means something about the eternity of God, and the all-sufficiency of God, and the omniscience of God. All of that is true, but when it comes to what God was doing, He was giving Moses a blank cheque—I AM. "Moses, do you need love? I AM love. Do you need power? I AM power. Do you need grace? I Am grace. Do you need humility? I AM your humility. Do you need strength? I AM your strength. Do you need wisdom?

I AM your wisdom. Do you need direction? I AM your direction. Moses, Moses, I AM in you! I AM in you! Yes, I AM all that you need in you, Moses. Go to Pharaoh and My purpose will be fulfilled," (see Exodus chapter 3).

But Moses was so much the old dried-up thorn bush that he said, "Lord, I stammer." He never thought of that before. "Lord, I stammer. I cannot speak." The Lord had such mercy upon Moses that He said, "Take Aaron your brother and he will do all the talking." Ever afterwards Moses did all the talking and Aaron did all the working. God knows how to humour us when He does His work so well that at the end we ourselves have no confidence in ourselves, not in a single atom of ourselves.

Do you begin to understand how wonderful this is? I used to wonder when I was young in the Lord why the Lord did not choose a palm tree and a wonderful blaze of glory at the top of some majestic, stately palm tree! The Lord would look down and say, "Moses, Moses, don't you come near here; this is holy ground." Wouldn't it have been wonderful? Especially if the palm tree is a symbol of righteousness and majesty.

Or suppose the Lord had spoken out of an acacia tree, that most beautiful and delicate of all trees of the desert. We Bible expositors would have had such a wonderful time with it. We would have said, "Now, you see the tabernacle, the Lord's dwelling place. He was in the acacia, (the shittim tree, in your old version). The Lord is in it, you see?" But He took a dried-up old thorn bush. Before ever you can become a palm tree, by the grace of God you must first be a dried-up old thorn bush. Before ever you can become an acacia, the material for the building of God's house, you must first know that you are a dried-up old thorn bush. God is the fire. You are the thorn bush.

But Moses saw more than that. He saw by the eyes of his heart, this is Israel. This old thorn bush is Israel and God is saying, "I, the living God, am in the midst of My people. I AM. I will be the pillar of cloud by day and the pillar of fire by night. I will be the manna from heaven. I will be water out of the rock. I will lead them all the way through. I will be a dwelling place. I will make them My dwelling place on earth. Moses, never forget that My people are nothing other than a dried-up old thorn bush. If you put your hand in you will get scratched." Oh, Moses found that out very quickly. Oh, how they murmured, how they rebelled, how they backbit, how they were all the time this and that. Nothing ever pleased them. They were a thorn bush. One time Moses got so angry that he struck the rock twice and said, "You rebels, shall I always bring water out of the rock for you?"

We must have the greatest sympathy with dear Moses. Those of us who work amongst the people of God, many times we would have struck the rock not once but ten times and said, "You rebels, we always have to bring the Word of God to you. All you do is gossip and backbite, devour one another and murmur, and nothing is ever right." Because of that one failure God said to him, "Moses, you have forgotten. You have forgotten. They are the thorn bush. Moses, I am the fire and you have touched Me. It was not your business to say what I did not give you to say. I am in this thorn bush; it is holy ground. Take off your shoes from your feet."

Remember that, dear child of God, when next you criticize some child of God, when you do injury to them, when you despitefully use them. Remember, you may hear the voice of God coming to you: "This is holy ground, this thorn bush. I am in it."

Paul Saw the Lord

So we can go on and on through the whole Bible. The apostle Paul saw the Lord on the road to Damascus (see Acts chapter 9). Many people think of that as some dramatic picture that he saw of the Lord. When the Lord said to him, "Saul, Saul, why persecutest thou me?" You will remember that Saul said, "Sir, who are You?" The Lord said, "I AM Jesus whom thou persecutest." Now because most Christians know their Bibles superficially, these statements run off them like water off a duck's back. Have you ever thought about it for one moment? Jesus was already dead as far as Paul was concerned, and suddenly he was struck down and a light shone above as the brightness of the sun at midday. Out of that brightness the apostle Paul heard the voice of God: "Saul, Saul, why persecutest thou me?" Saul said, "Who are You? Who are You?" The Lord said, "Jesus." Then Saul said, "But Lord I am not persecuting You; You are dead. You have long since gone. I am persecuting those wretched people that have made an extreme fanatical sect out of Your teaching."

Do you see what happened? On that day the apostle Paul saw the Lord, maybe only dimly, but in the three years that he was in Arabia perhaps it became more clearly to him. He saw that the Lord Jesus' people were His members. They were part of Him, and when you struck them, you struck the Lord. When you injured them, you injured the Lord. Out of that vision came all of Paul's ministry. He said in Galatians 1 (see verses 15–16):

"When it pleased the Lord to reveal His Son in me." Later on when he talked about the body of Christ and being in Christ, I believe it all came from that heavenly vision. The apostle Paul said in the end, "Wherefore O King Agrippa, I was not disobedient to the heavenly vision" (Acts 26:19).

Do I begin to make you see that this matter of vision is all-important? You can go to a theological seminary for ten years and it will kill you. You can go to Bible course after Bible course, but if you do not have vision then the whole thing is just knowledge and knowledge puffeth up; only love builds up. There is, of course, the right kind of knowledge; I am not just attacking knowledge. There is the knowledge of the Lord—that I may know Him. Or what the apostle Paul meant when he said that the Lord may give unto you the Spirit of wisdom and revelation in the knowledge of Him, the eyes of your heart being enlightened that you may know—not know about Him but know Him (Ephesians 1:17b).

Dear family of God, there have been many, many things that we have talked about in these last days. What a need there is for vision! Everything will be lost in this time if in the end God does not give us that vision of Himself. We need to see the greatness of the Lord! We live in days of small things. Christ is so small—we can reduce Him to a formula. We can reduce Him to a certain number of methods, a technique. We can make Him somehow or other just a creed. Oh, if only we saw the Lord and we could see the greatness of the Lord! He is not contained in a teaching or a creed or an experience. Not even in one believer is all the fullness of our Lord contained. He is so infinite, so great. If we could only see the Lord.

Daniel Saw the Lord

When Daniel saw the Lord, he fell down as one dead. When Ezekiel saw the Lord, he fell down as one dead. When John saw the Lord, he fell down as one dead. Oh, this kind of vision is not the kind of vision that sends people on a world tour to tell people all around the world about the vision they had. God forbid! This kind of vision is the death of the person who sees it. For when they see the Lord in all His infinity and greatness and mercy and love, it is as if they die in His presence and the Lord has to come and set them up on their feet. Have you ever noticed that? Again and again in the Bible when people see the Lord, they fall at His feet as dead and someone has to come and set them up and put their right hand on them and say, "Fear not." Have you ever had such a vision? Every time we see the Lord, we feel we know nothing. Every time we see the greatness of the Lord, we feel as though we are so small and so little and that it is impossible. It is as if we die. Oh, to see the greatness of the Lord!

Isaiah Saw the Lord

In the year that King Uzziah died, when Isaiah was in the temple praying and worshipping, he suddenly saw the Lord high and lifted up (Isaiah 6:1). He could no longer see the temple. He could not see the sanctuary for the sense of the Lord praying, filled and enveloped the whole sanctuary.

May God give us such a vision of the Lord that we do not see the things around us but we see Him. In the end everything is in Him. People make the church a doctrine. They make it a detached thing. Here is the Lord; there is the church. But in essence the church is Christ. It is being one body in Him. It is growing into a holy temple in the Lord, being built together as a home of God in the Spirit. It is all in the Lord. If we could see that it would save us so much.

It is a wonderful thing when we see our salvation as our Saviour. It is not just that He has finished the work, thank God for that; it is the legal side of our salvation. But the subjective and glorious side is that He is our Saviour who ever lives to make intercession for us. If we have been reconciled through His death, how much more shall we be saved through His life. Oh, what a wonderful thing it is when the Lord gets that inside of us. We are born of God, and we find that our salvation is not a thing; it is a Person.

It is a wonderful thing when we find our sanctification is a Person. People talk of holiness as if it is an experience, a second blessing. Thank God, there is such an experience of our Lord, but it is all the Lord. I had an experience. How? When I saw that I had been crucified with Christ. I died with Him and was buried with Him. Those of you who have been baptized and made alive together with Him to walk in newness of life, that is an experience of a Person. That is a Person.

Some people make so much of the baptism of the Holy Spirit. I believe there is an anointing of the Spirit. I would die on that point. I do not want to cause division or confusion, but I am sure there is an experience of anointing for service, and we need to know it as soon as we are saved, the sooner the better. I know some people, thank God, who entered into it right at the moment they were saved. What a wonderful thing it is to know the anointing, but the anointing is not a thing. People are all the time looking for an experience that knocks them out or bowls them over, where somehow or other they go into ecstasies and all the rest of it. I thank God for those of us who have had an ecstasy or two. In this poor world it is something to have an ecstasy. I do not begrudge anyone having an ecstasy. If you are caught up to the third heaven and see the Lord, praise God, as long as you keep your mouth shut when you come down, and do not go around making such a thing of it all the time that it becomes sort of crazied.

The Lord Jesus is the baptizer in the Holy Spirit. The only way I was born of the Spirit was through the Lord Jesus. The only way the Holy Spirit came to dwell in me was by the Lord Jesus. The only way that I can be anointed with the Holy Spirit and power is through the Lord Jesus. It is not that I am good enough, or that I have merits or anything else. It is the work of my Lord that brings me into the anointing. It is all of grace.

Many people have asked me about the comment I made about an anointing for a meeting. That would be a subject all on its own about anointing—how to stay in the anointing, how to abide under the anointing, how to distinguish it. Dear child of God, the anointing is in Christ. The oil is upon the Head, even Aaron's head, and runs down upon his beard and down to the hem of his garment and includes every member of the body (see Psalm 133). My anointing is the Lord Jesus. He has obtained something for me and poured forth this which you see and hear, and so it could go on. Whatever it is, whether it is some experience of the Lord, some moving on with the Lord, it is all in Him, and we need to see it. May the Lord give us such vision. *May the Lord give us such vision.*

God's Means of Apprehending a Person

Then I would like to close by saying something about the way God apprehends us through vision. How does God take hold of a person? How does He arrest a person? How does He apprehend a person? It is always through vision. Through such vision we are apprehended of the Lord.

Once the apostle Paul saw the Lord, he had no time for anything petty. In Philippians 3 he said some incredible things. If I had written the Roman letter, I would be insufferable! If I had written, even by the grace of God, I and II Corinthians, Galatians, I and II Thessalonians, and possibly Philemon, apart from Ephesians and Colossians, which some think are almost the last of Timothy, I would be opening Bible colleges, running a theological seminary, conducting Bible study courses, and all the rest of it. I would not be saying, "I count everything but loss that I may win Christ." I would say to the apostle Paul, "Paul, you are such an exaggerator. Win Christ? But you already have Christ. Paul, wake up! You already have Christ. Who got hold of you on the road to Damascus?" Why, he would say, "The Lord." "But Paul you are clothed with the righteousness of Christ." "Of course, I am clothed with the righteousness of Christ." "But Paul, you wrote Romans. If you had only written that one letter you obviously have won Christ. Think of the 12th chapter of Corinthians! Think of the 13th chapter of Corinthians! Think of the 15th chapter of Corinthians! If I had written just one of those I would feel that I had done my job, and I would sit down on a flowery bed of ease and wait to go to glory. I would think: "Well, I have done my part. What I have given is Scripture.

But Paul, you have written Galatians and Thessalonians and even talked in II Corinthians chapter 12 of being caught up to the third heaven and hearing things that are not lawful for a man to utter." I think that is the proper spiritual experience. To come back and say I have had something from the Lord and I am going to tell you. That is one great thing, isn't it? But to be able to come and say, "I heard something that I am not allowed to tell you." That is the climax of all spiritual experience. Then you are really, as it were, *in*. You are in the spiritual Pentagon.

The apostle Paul had so seen the greatness of the Lord and the infinity of the Lord, that forever afterwards he just knew how much he did not know. When you are a student, you think you know everything. You can dogmatically hold forth on this and that and the other, but when you get a university professor, you find He is much more careful. He says, "It could be this or it could be that, but I think it is probably this." Why? It is because he knows so much more. The student knows so much less and therefore can be dogmatic, but the professor knows so much more and therefore knows that he knows so little. In other words, he knows that there is so much more to know.

Have you come there yet? I feel sorry for Christians who know it all. They say, "I have the Lord. I'll introduce Him to you—point one, two, three, and four. Do you want an experience of the Holy Spirit? Five steps; come to me. I will give you five steps and you will be in. Do you want an experience of holiness? Well, come to me. I have seven steps here."

Oh, when somehow or other we have seen the greatness of the Lord, it is as if we know how much more there is to know. We know how little we really know. It is as if we are put to sea on an infinite ocean, and the more we go out into the ocean the smaller the vessel becomes and the greater the horizon. That is what vision does for you. Vision will always make you feel little and God infinite. It will always make you know how tiny you are and how fathomless God is. But vision will also make you know that God's infinity and your finiteness are linked together eternally. His fullness and your littleness are one; the old thorn bush and the fire of God have come together forever. That is vision.

The Measure of Vision

The measure of our vision will determine just how far we go. Some people have only seen the matter of salvation, and that is as far as they will go. They will be perfectly happy about only evangelistic things. Thank God for people who have an evangelistic burden! Never think it is kindergarten as if by going on with the Lord you leave that kind of thing behind. God forbid! We have a commission from the Lord to make disciples of all nations. Woe betide any company that has no outreach. They will die because they have not got the passion of their Lord in them. But having said that, if you only see salvation that is as far as you will go. If you see a bit more, maybe the charismatic, that is as far as you will go and that will be the limit of it. You will always be trying to get people into an experience, full stop. Or maybe you have seen something more and you are always trying to get someone into more. You have seen something about the second coming of the Lord. You are great on prophecy, so you are always trying to get people to understand that. But if we see the purpose of the Lord concerning the Lord Jesus and those who are in Him that will determine how far we go. It is without limit.

Vision Disturbs

May I say something else? Vision always disturbs. I will say that again. *Vision always disturbs.* People seem to think that if you have a vision suddenly you are set up. You have got it now. You can get on the platform and start like a tape recorder. Press the button and out it comes, and they all sit with their mouths open listening to these wonderful words pouring out of your mouth. My dear friend, any man or woman who is given real vision is a disturbed person. Abraham went out. He could not stay in Ur a moment longer. Moses went in. He could not stay in the desert a moment longer. He had to go into Pharaoh's house. Daniel got so disturbed that for three weeks he started on the prayer ministry, and oh my, what a battle he got into! Great principalities and powers stopping the angel coming along with the answer for Daniel. Vision always disturbs. Paul could not settle for anything little. If you ask God for vision just remember what you are asking for. You are asking for spiritual disturbance. Some of you who are quite happy to be denominational may find that suddenly you get very disturbed—not bitter and not superior, but disturbed. Some of you, who are in other things that have gone right off the rails, will find that if God gives you real vision you are going to get disturbed. You will have to ask yourself: If the lampstand goes, where do I go? Vision always disturbs.

Vision Leads to Burden and Travail

Vision leads to burden and travail. Have you ever noticed how so many of the prophets speak of their prophecy as the burden of the Lord because they saw the Lord. It is travail. Some of you have spoken to me about travail. It begins with vision. No one will ever be trusted with travail who has not seen the Lord. Oh my dear friends, I hope I have said enough in this closing time to make you realise that I reckon that all that has been ministered is futile unless God grants to you a spirit of wisdom and revelation in the knowledge of Himself. That is not sensational or dramatic necessarily, but suddenly what you thought you dimly perceived with your brain, comes with a flash in your heart, and for the first time you begin to see something. That which you begin to see, you will see more and more clearly as you go on with the Lord.

Vision Produces Ministry

For you brethren whom God is using, vision produces ministry. Do you want the real ministry of the Word and not just one of those structured, systemized ministries, but a real ministry of the Word? It comes out of vision. Daniel saw the Lord and out of it came ministry both in prayer, in travail, and in word. Ezekiel saw the Lord and out of it came a tremendous ministry. Isaiah saw the Lord and out of it came one of the greatest ministries to the people of the old covenant and we in the new have ever received. John saw the Lord and out of that came the book of Revelation. Paul saw the Lord and out of it came his tremendous ministry. All ministry in the end comes out of vision.

There are many other things that vision does. It creates living faith. When we see the Lord, faith comes into our hearts. The God of glory appeared unto our father Abraham, and by faith he obeyed to go out not knowing whither he went. Faith changes us into the likeness of our wonderful Lord, for as we behold His glory as in a mirror, so we are changed into the same image from glory to glory even as from the Lord the Spirit (see II Corinthians 3:18).

Dear child of God, we need to see the Lord, and in the end the permanent effect and value of these days will be precisely in the measure in which we see the Lord. Moses saw the Lord again and again and again. He saw the Lord in such a way as no other human being has really seen the Lord, and yet (this has always captured me), when the Lord asked Moses: "Is there anything you want?" He said, "Show me Thy glory," (Exodus 33:18). That is the evidence of a man who has begun to see the Lord, for when you begin to see the Lord, you want more. I think many of us would have been satisfied with what Moses had already seen and heard; but not Moses. For this is what vision always does. We find that we have to go on with Him.

Shall we pray?

Our beloved Lord, we do praise Thee that Thou art the One who alone can give vision to Thy people. Oh Lord, in this matter Thou hast shut us up to Thyself. We cannot get that from a Bible study course or outline, or a Bible college or even in a conference as such. Lord, Thou art the only One who can give to Thy people that Spirit of wisdom and revelation in the knowledge of Thy Son. Oh Lord, awaken us all to this matter and may there be drawn out of all our hearts a yearning and a longing to see the Lord. Translate all these things that have been ministered over these days through whomsoever Thou hast used. Translate all these things into reality through revelation. Oh God, touch the eyes of our heart and show us Thy glory. So together we commit ourselves to Thee in the name of our Lord Jesus Christ. Amen.

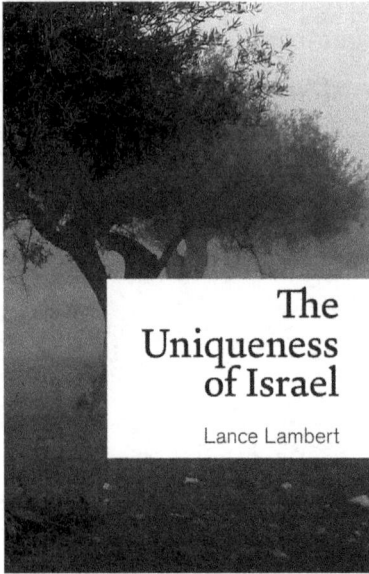

The
Uniqueness
of Israel

Lance Lambert

The Uniqueness of Israel

Woven into the fabric of Jewish existence there is an undeniable uniqueness. There is bitter controversy over the subject of Israel, but time itself will establish the truth about this nation's place in God's plan. For Lance Lambert, the Lord Jesus is the key that unlocks Jewish history He is the key not only to their fall, but also to their restoration. For in spite of the fact that they rejected Him, He has not rejected them.

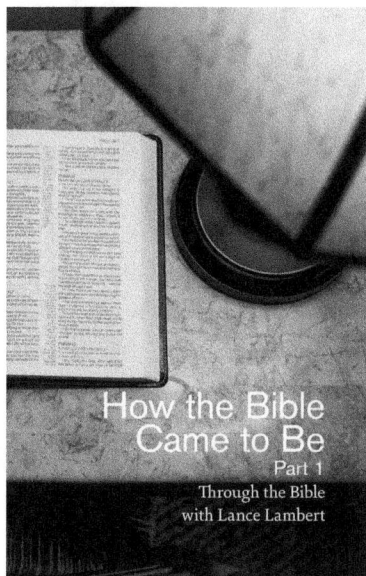

How the Bible Came to Be

How is the Bible still as applicable in the 21st century as it was when it was first penned? How did so many authors, with different backgrounds and over thousands of years, write something so perfectly fitting with one another?

Lance Lambert breaks down these, and many other questions in this first volume of his series teaching through the Bible. He lays a firm foundation for going on to study the Word of the living God.

And ye shall seek me, and find me, when ye shall
search for me with all your heart. Jeremiah 29:13

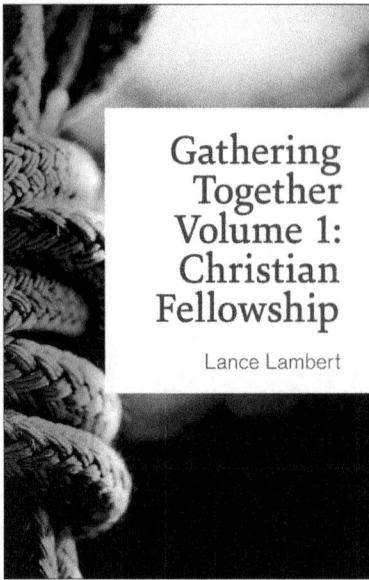

Gathering Together Volume 1: Christian Fellowship

What is the church?

What is the basis for meeting together as the church?

What is true fellowship?

What is the priesthood of all believers?

What is the difference between unity and uniformity in the church?

In the first volume of *Gathering Together*, Lance Lambert answers these questions and many more. In doing this, he emphasizes the absolute headship of Christ and the oneness of the body of Christ.

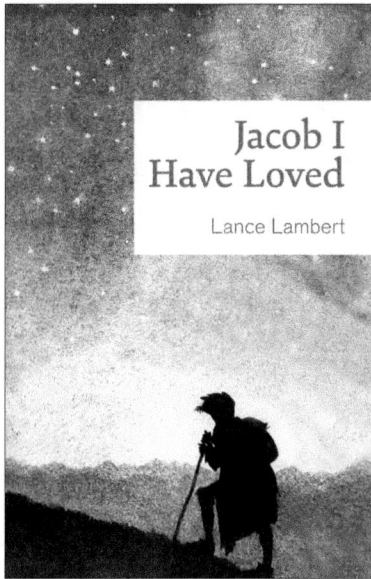

Jacob I Have Loved

When God deals with us it is often in deeply mystifying ways. There is no greater example of how God shapes a person than through the remarkable story of Jacob. Jacob I Have Loved is an outstanding illustration of God's desire to utterly transform our fallen inner nature. Despite a twisted, deceiving, and sinful heart, Jacob nonetheless inherited God's richest blessings and became one of the patriarchs of our faith. Herein lies one of the Bible's great mysteries. His story is an integral part of the history of divine redemption. This book is about the power of God to transform a human life.

Jacob's story is our story.

www.ingramcontent.com/pod-product-compliance
Lightning Source LLC
LaVergne TN
LVHW051256080426
835509LV00020B/2999